Why Fish Don't Exist

A Story of Loss, Love,
and the Hidden Order of Life

Lulu Miller

Illustrations by Kate Samworth

SIMON & SCHUSTER

NEW YORK   LONDON   TORONTO   SYDNEY   NEW DELHI

Simon & Schuster
1230 Avenue of the Americas
New York, NY 10020

First Simon & Schuster hardcover edition April 2020

SIMON & SCHUSTER and colophon are registered trademarks of Simon & Schuster, Inc.

For information about special discounts for bulk purchases, please contact Simon & Schuster Special Sales at 1-866-506-1949 or business@simonandschuster.com.

The Simon & Schuster Speakers Bureau can bring authors to your live event. For more information or to book an event, contact the Simon & Schuster Speakers Bureau at 1-866-248-3049 or visit our website at www.simonspeakers.com.

Interior design by Carly Loman

Manufactured in the United States of America

10 9 8 7 6 5 4 3 2 1

Library of Congress Cataloging-in-Publication Data has been applied for.

ISBN 978-1-5011-6027-1
ISBN 978-1-5011-6037-0 (ebook)

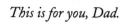

This is for you, Dad.

Contents

Why Fish Don't Exist

Prologue

icture the person you love the most. Picture them sitting on the couch, eating cereal, ranting about something totally charming, like how it bothers them when people sign their emails with a single initial instead of taking those four extra keystrokes to just finish the job—

Chaos will get them.

Chaos will crack them from the outside—with a falling branch, a speeding car, a bullet—or unravel them from the inside, with the mutiny of their very own cells. Chaos will rot your plants and kill your dog and rust your bike. It will decay your most precious memories, topple your favorite cities, wreck any sanctuary you can ever build.

It's not if, it's when. Chaos is the only sure thing in this world. The master that rules us all. My scientist father taught me early that there is no escaping the Second Law of Thermodynamics: entropy is only growing; it can never be diminished, no matter what we do.

A smart human accepts this truth. A smart human does not try to fight it.

But one spring day in 1906, a tall American man with a walrus mustache dared to challenge our master.

His name was David Starr Jordan, and in many ways, it was his day job to fight Chaos. He was a taxonomist, the kind of scientist charged with bringing order to the Chaos of the earth by uncovering the shape of the great tree of life—that branching map said to reveal how all plants and animals are interconnected. His specialty was fish, and he spent his days sailing the globe in search of new species. New clues that he hoped would reveal more about nature's hidden blueprint.

For years he worked, for decades, so tirelessly that he and his crew would eventually discover a full *fifth* of fish known to man in his day. By the thousand he reeled in new species, dreaming up names for them, punching those names into shiny tin tags, dropping the tags alongside their specimens into jars of ethanol, slowly stacking his discoveries higher and higher.

Until one spring morning in 1906, an earthquake struck and toppled his shimmering collection to the ground.

Hundreds of jars shattered against the floor. His fish specimens were mutilated by broken glass and fallen shelves. But worst of all were the *names*. Those carefully placed tin tags had been launched at random all over the ground. In some terrible act of Genesis in reverse, his thousands of meticulously named fish had transformed back into a heaping mass of the unknown.

But as he stood there in the wreckage, his life's work eviscerated at his feet, this mustachioed scientist did something strange. He didn't give up or despair. He did not heed what seemed to be the clear message of the quake: that in a world ruled by Chaos, any attempts at order are doomed to fail eventually. Instead, he rolled up his sleeves and scrambled around until he found, of all the weapons in the world, a sewing needle.

He took the needle between his thumb and forefinger, laced it with thread, and aimed it at one of the few fish he recognized amid the destruction. With one fluid movement, he plunged the needle through the flesh at the fish's throat. Then he used the trailing thread to stitch a name tag directly to the flesh itself.

For each fish he could salvage, he repeated this tiny gesture. No longer would he let the tin tags sit precariously in the jars. Instead, he sewed each name directly to the creature's skin. A name stitched to its throat. To its tail. To its eyeball. It was a small innovation with a defiant wish, that his work would now be protected against the onslaughts of Chaos, that his order would stand tall next time she struck.

When I first heard about David Starr Jordan's attack on Chaos, I was in my early twenties, starting out as a science reporter. Instantly, I assumed he was a fool. The needle might work against a quake, but what about fire or flood or rust or any of the trillion modes of destruction he hadn't thought to consider? His innovation with the sewing needle seemed so flimsy, so shortsighted, so magnificently unaware of the forces that ruled him. He seemed to me a lesson in hubris. An Icarus of the fish collection.

But as I grew older, as Chaos had her way with me, as I made a wreck of my own life and began to try to piece it back together, I started to wonder about this taxonomist. Maybe he had figured something out—about persistence, or purpose, or how to go on—that I needed to know. Maybe it was okay to have some outsized faith in yourself. Maybe plunging along in complete denial of your doomed chances was not the mark of a fool but—it felt sinful to think it—a victor?

So, one wintry afternoon when I was feeling particularly hopeless, I typed the name *David Starr Jordan* into Google and was met with a sepia photograph of an old white man with a bushy walrus mustache. His eyes looked a little hard.

Who are you? I wondered. *A cautionary tale? Or a model of how to be?*

I clicked through to more pictures of him. There he was as a boy, suddenly lamblike, with spilling dark curls and protruding ears. There he was as a young man, standing upright in a rowboat. His shoulders had filled out and he was biting his lower lip in a way that could almost be classified as sultry. There he was as a grandfatherly old man, sitting in an armchair, scratching a shaggy, white dog. I saw links to articles and books he had written. Fish-collecting guides, taxonomic studies of the fishes of Korea, of Samoa, of Panama. But there were also essays about drinking and humor and meaning and despair. He had written children's books and satires and poems and, best of all, for the lost journalist seeking guidance in the lives of others, an out-of-print memoir called *The Days of a Man*, packed tight with so many details about said days of said man it had to be broken into two volumes. It was nearly a century out of print, but I found a used-book dealer who would sell it to me for $27.99.

When the package arrived, it felt warm, enchanted. As if it contained a treasure map. I slid a steak knife through the packing tape, and two olive-green tomes spilled out, each glittering with gold letters. I made a huge pot of coffee and sat down on the couch, the first volume on my lap, ready to find out what becomes of you when you refuse to surrender to Chaos.

1.

A Boy with His Head in the Stars

avid Jordan was born on an apple orchard in upstate New York in 1851 at the darkest time of the year, which is perhaps why he became so preoccupied with the stars. "While husking corn on autumn evenings," he writes of his boyhood, "I became curious as to the names and significance of the celestial bodies." He could not just enjoy their twinkling; he found them a mess he needed ordered, known. When he was about eight years old, he got his hands on an atlas of astronomical charts and began comparing what he saw on the page to what he saw above his head. Night by night he went, creeping out of the house, attempting to learn the name of every star in the sky. And according to him, it took only five years to bring order to the entire night sky. As a reward, he chose "Starr" as his middle name, and wore it proudly for the rest of his life.

Having mastered the celestial, David Starr Jordan turned to the terrestrial. His family's land swelled and rolled with its own unique constellations of trees, boulders, farm buildings, and livestock. His parents kept him busy with chores, shearing the sheep, clearing brush, and—David's specialty—sewing rags into rugs (his flexor tendons learning early how to wield a needle). But in between chores, David began to map the land.

For help, he turned to his big brother, Rufus, thirteen years older, a quiet and gentle nature lover with deep brown eyes. Rufus taught David how to settle the horses, with long strokes down the neck, where in the thickets to find the juiciest blueberries. Watching Rufus demystify the earth, David was transfixed; he says he held Rufus in "absolute worship." Slowly, David began drawing intricate maps of everything they saw. He drew maps of his family's orchard, his walk to school, and when he finished the land he knew, he turned to places far away. He copied charts of distant townships, states, countries, continents, until his hungry little fingers had crawled over nearly every corner of the globe.

"The eagerness I then displayed," he writes, "rather worried my mother," a large woman named Huldah. One day, having had enough, she took his whole pile of maps, creased and stained with his boyish sweat, and chucked it.

Why? Who knows. Perhaps it was because Huldah and her husband, Hiram, were devout Puritans. They prided themselves on martyr-y accomplishments like never laughing out loud and beating the sun to the fields each morning. Spending one's time making maps of lands already mapped would have seemed like a frivolity, an insult to the use of a day, especially when they were struggling as they were, when there were apples to pick and potatoes to hoe and rags to sew.

Or perhaps Huldah's disapproval was simply a reflection of the times. By the mid-nineteenth century, the obsessive ordering of the natural world was beginning to fall out of fashion. The Age of Discovery had started over four hundred years before, and pretty much wrapped up in 1758, when the father of modern taxonomy, Carl Linnaeus, finished his masterpiece, *Systema Naturae*, a proposed blueprint for all the interconnections of life. (No matter that Linnaeus's chart was riddled with mistakes: misfiling bats as primates and sea urchins as worms, to name a couple.) As boats raced more frequently from port to port, the excitement of glimpsing exotic specimens and maps—once a way of luring people into shops, taverns, coffeehouses—was wearing off. Dust was collecting upon cabinets of curiosity; the world, it seemed, had become known.

Though there's a chance it could have been something else. At that very moment, a blasphemous text was screeching through the presses. *On the Origin of Species* was released to the masses in 1859, just as little David was beginning to scrunch his nose up at the stars. Is there any possibility that Huldah could have read the newspapers, could have sensed that the order of the natural world was about to cave in?

Whatever the reason, Huldah would not budge. With her fist full of David's crumpled maps, she told her son to find something "more relevant" to do with his time.

Like a good boy, he obeyed: he stopped making maps. But like a real boy, he did not. Not really.

"The country round about my home was very rich in wild flowers," he writes, trying to blame the earth for his sin. On his way home from school he began to ever so occasionally pluck a velvety blue pom-pom or silken orange star from the grass. Some he'd sniff and let fall to the ground, but occasionally one would linger in his fingers and make it back to his bedroom, where it would lie on the bed and taunt him with its mysterious arrangement of petals. He would try to suppress this desire to know it, its name, its exact location on the tree of life. And he did pretty well, until puberty hit.

On his first day of middle school, David secreted home from the library "a little book on flowers." And back in the privacy of his room, he'd sit, manual in hand, desk dirty with flowers, discerning which flower was which, unbuttoning its genus, its species. A near man now, with some hair on his toes, his voice dropping, he'd occasionally taunt his mother by revealing the scientific names of the blossoms they walked by—transmuting periwinkles into *Vinca major* or sunflowers into *Helianthus annuus*—as though to say that this passion of his could not be swatted out of him, crumpled up or thrown away. "I perhaps strained a point by adorning the conveniently white walls of my bedroom with the names of the different plants as I identified them in turn," he writes.

He began keeping questionable company, with a poor farmer up the road named Joshua Ellenwood who had learned the scientific name of almost every plant in the region. For accomplishing such a feat, the old man was regarded by his neighbors as "shiftless and a waster of time."

David was in awe of him. He began trailing the old man on his walks through the countryside, trying to seep up as many of his tricks as possible—the ways species revealed themselves in leaf shape or petal count or aroma. After meeting Joshua, David renounced his love of beauty, declaring that the dull and ugly flowers—the dandelions (*Taraxacum officinale*) and buttercups (*Ranunculus acris*)—held better clues to nature's blueprint. "The little ones," he wrote, "even though not beautiful, meant more to me than a hundred big ones all of a kind. A special proof of scientific as distinguished from aesthetic interest is to care for the hidden and insignificant."

The hidden and insignificant.

Could David be revealing something about himself in there? Though he doesn't let on to it much in his memoir, the human world could be hard on him. The historian Edward McNall Burns writes that when David's parents enrolled him in a boarding school, "the girls did not consider [him] too promising, for it is said that other young males were sometimes hauled up at night [to the girls' dorm] in a basket intended to be used for elevating fuel." David, alas, never once got to experience the miracle of basket flight.

As he grew up, the outside world seemed to grow harsher. He

writes of skating out onto an ice pond only to get in a tussle with a boy much smaller than him, of trying to sing but being told to quit by his music teacher, of the baseball game he joined at the age of sixteen that ended abruptly when he dove for a fly ball and was "led off with a broken nose, which, being badly set, has ever since remained slightly askew." And then there was his first teaching gig, his pupils a group of unruly boys in a nearby town. For weeks David attempted to maintain some semblance of order by conducting class with a wooden pointer; he'd wave it around, trying to focus their attention, occasionally even whapping the worst of the boys with it. Until, that is, the boys revolted. They descended upon David, grabbed his trusty pointer, and set it on fire.

He writes of turning to more solitary pleasures—reading adventure stories and poetry, consuming himself with the task of trying to "clasp [my] hands and jump through them." But even in solitude he wasn't safe. One day, when David was eleven years old and happily "engaged in the congenial task of burning stumps," his older sister, Lucia, appeared at the doorway to their farmhouse, screaming, as he recalls it, "that if I wanted to see my brother alive I must hurry to the house."

David was confused. Rufus wasn't even supposed to be home. A passionate abolitionist, he had recently left to enlist in the Union army. But before getting to set foot on the battlefield, before getting to test the strength of his conviction, Rufus had contracted a mysterious illness in training camp. It was a sickness that moved quickly through his body, raising his temperature and boiling his skin with rose-colored spots—a disease with no known cause or cure in those days, called, simply, "army fever." (Decades later it would be named typhus.)

When David reached his brother's bedside, Rufus's compass-like eyes were lolling and loose, barely able to focus. David stayed by the bed for hours, willing the fates to restore some strength to his brother's body.

The next morning, Rufus did not wake.

"I still remember the long period of loneliness and distress after his untimely death," David writes. "Night after night I would dream that it was not true and that he had returned safe and sound."

After Rufus's death, David's journals explode with color. Meticulously rendered sketches of wildflowers and ferns and ivies and brambles and any scraps of nature, it seemed, he could tear away from the world. The drawings are not artful; they are labored, covered in pencil smudges, ink stains, eraser marks, and little tears from overly vigorous coloring in. But in the crudeness you can see it—his obsession, his desperation, the near-muscular effort he was exerting to pin down the forms of the things unknown to him. Beneath each drawing there is, finally, a scientific name. The ink runs suddenly smoother, the letters looping with a bit of command. *Campanula rotundifolia. Kalmia glauca. Astragalus canadensis.* David describes the sensation of speaking the names out loud, those Latin declarations of victory, mastery. "Their appellations," he writes, "are as honey on my lips."

Psychologists have studied this, by the way, the sweet salve that collecting can offer in times of anguish. In *Collecting: An Unruly Passion*, psychologist Werner Muensterberger, who counseled compulsive collectors for decades, notes that the habit often kicks into high gear after some sort of "deprivation or loss or vulnerability," with each new acquisition flooding the collector with an intoxicating burst of "fantasized omnipotence." Francisca López-Torrecillas, who has been studying collectors for years at the University of Granada, noted a similar phenomenon, that people experiencing stress or anxiety would turn to collecting to soothe their pain. "When people have this feeling of personal inefficiency," she writes, "compulsive collecting helps them in feeling better." The only danger, Muensterberger warns, is that—as with any compulsion—there seems to be a line where the habit can switch from "exhilarating" to "ruinous."

As David grew older, as his shoulders filled out and his lips plumped, his hunger for new specimens only intensified. But he couldn't seem to find anyone who cared. No matter how hard he studied, no matter how many new species names he learned or taxonomy papers he was able to get published, he explains, "at school no attention was paid to this interest of mine." He got into Cornell University, earning a bachelor's and master's degree in science in just three years. But he had trouble finding work. Universities were looking for sociable men in smartly tied ties who could command a classroom with a pointer and charm. The quiet, skinned-knee, dirty-elbowed crawling around in nature that David so loved was looked down upon as child's play.

And so it could have gone for David. Him, desperately driven to collect flowers. The world, unconvinced of his calling's worthiness. Time passing, as he slowly dug himself deeper and deeper into a leafy loneliness.

Had he not stepped foot on Penikese Island.

2.

A Prophet on an Island

enikese Island sits fourteen miles off the coast of Massachusetts. At just under a mile long, with barely any tree cover to protect from the beating sun, it has been called the "runt" of its island chain, a "sad and lonely little rock," and an "outpost of hell."

Yet for some reason, its naked shores have always been a spot where people have tried to cultivate hope. In the early 1900s, it was a leper colony led by a doctor who wanted to find a way to cure his wards. In the 1950s it was converted into a bird sanctuary where naturalists tried to reverse the fates of a plummeting tern population. In the 1970s, the island became a reform school for delinquent or wayward or troubled boys (the name depended on the decade), where a marine and fisherman hoped a regimen of seclusion, manual labor, animal husbandry, boatbuilding, communal living, and schoolwork could "turn a lot of potential murderers into car thieves." By the time I learned of the island, it had become a heroin recovery center, where people addicted to the drug could try to get clean once and for all. But before all that, back in David Starr Jordan's day, the group seeking salvation on the lonely little rock? Naturalists.

By 1873, when David was a freshly minted Cornell grad, one of the most famous naturalists of the day, Louis Agassiz, had grown gravely concerned about the future of the trade. Agassiz was a

Swiss geologist, a charismatic bear of a man with bushy mutton chops, who had earned his fame by being one of the earliest proponents of the ice age theory. Agassiz had only come to this vision of an earth coated in ice after making meticulous observations of fossils and scratch marks in the bedrock. As a result, he believed that the best way to teach science was to scrutinize nature. "Study nature, not books" was his motto, and he was known for locking his students in a closet with dead animals and not allowing them to emerge until they had discovered "all the truths which the objects contained."

In his forties, he took a job at Harvard and was troubled by what he found there. No digging around in the dirt, no students locked in closets with tiny rotting corpses. Just papers and tests and recitations regurgitating the beliefs printed in science books. This approach concerned Agassiz, who warned that "science, generally, hates beliefs." As late as the 1850s, for example, many respectable scientists still believed in the idea of "spontaneous generation"— the belief that fleas and maggots could spring forth from particles of dust; a few decades before that, scientists believed in a magical substance called "phlogiston" that determined whether or not a material would burn; at that very moment, people had no way of protecting their loved ones against mysterious illnesses like "army fever"—bacteria having not yet been discovered as the cause of that disease. No, if you were satisfied with the beliefs of the day, Agassiz worried, it kept you stunted, stymied, sick. The way out, the way to enlightenment, was to keep looking, closer, longer, at the pebbles and petals and pelts of this world.

So, Agassiz dreamed of creating a safe haven where he could right this wrong, a kind of summer camp for young naturalists where he could teach the art of direct observation out in nature. And when, in 1873, a wealthy landowner offered to donate Penikese Island to the cause, he jumped at the opportunity.

Its location was ideal: an hour from the mainland, easy enough to access, yet far enough to feel free. So was its size: big enough to roam, but small enough to never get lost. And as for the subjects available for study on Penikese? Well, where to begin. Coating its treeless shores was a lush carpet of seagrass, which whipped in the wind and rustled with treasures—crabs, dragonflies, snakes, mice, crickets, plovers, beetles, owls. There were also the tide pools, silty with snails and seaweed and barnacles. And perhaps Agassiz's favorite, the big blond boulders scattered like clunky teeth all over the island, some of them over fifteen feet tall, which revealed in their scratch marks the direction the mighty glacier had been traveling some twenty thousand years before. Finally, there was the lovely lapping sea itself. A sapphire platter that offered endless riches—sea stars, jellies, oysters, urchins, rays, horseshoe crabs, sea squirts, bioluminescence, and fish after glorious, slimy, shimmering fish. The naturalists' nets would never come up empty. For a person hoping to teach using nature itself, the place was a gold mine.

As Agassiz began shipping lumber to the island to construct the camp, David Starr Jordan sat halfway across the country in Galesburg, Illinois, reading the newspaper. He had finally landed a job, teaching science at a small Christian university called Lombard College. But he was miserable. He felt isolated geographically and spiritually. His colleagues criticized him for teaching the blasphemous ice age theory, and worse, for allowing his students to handle lab instruments and "waste chemicals." It was cold in Illinois and the earth was flat and he missed the flowering gorges of his youth. But one dark morning in early spring, he flipped the page of his newspaper and came across an ad for a "Course of Instruction in Natural History to Be Delivered by the Seaside" by none other than Louis Agassiz himself.

I picture David snarfing his morning coffee out his nose—but it wouldn't have been coffee, because he was a lifelong teetotaler (eschewing not just booze and tobacco but even caffeine, for its dangerous ability to alter perception). So perhaps he snarfed water, snarfed herbal tea, snarfed something in disbelief that such a place could exist. He applied to the camp as fast as he could. Within weeks, the mail brought his letter of acceptance, his ticket out of Illinois, signed by Agassiz's very own hand.

Just a few months later, on July 8, 1873, David Starr Jordan stepped onto a pier in New Bedford, Massachusetts, and beheld the ocean for the very first time. He was twenty-two years old.

Slowly, more and more young naturalists began gathering beside him on the dock, a mix of young men and women. It was a beautiful morning. The bay was calm, the sky a brilliant blue. A tugboat was headed their way, ready to shuttle them off to the faraway speck on the horizon. The boat threw down its planks and the fifty young naturalists walked aboard. It's lost to time what the campers talked about as they chugged into the waves. Maybe they exchanged tall tales about the fauna of their homelands, asked one another to which kingdom they pledged their allegiance: animal, vegetable, or mineral. Maybe, if asked, David would have replied with one of his trustiest jokes, that due to the dense ivy that overtook the walls of his boyhood home, he became a "botanist in self-defense." Or perhaps he stayed glued to the boat's railing, scanning those rolling gray waves for slips of skin; he confessed to a lingering shyness in those years, a wariness of new places; perhaps he consoled himself with that age-old technique of finding refuge in nature.

About an hour later, the tugboat shifted its engines into a lower gear and began its approach to the island. From his spot on the deck, David could make out the silhouette of a long dock with a human standing at the tip. He writes:

None of us will ever forget his first sight of Agassiz. We had come down from New Bedford in a little tug-boat in the early morning, and Agassiz met us at the landing-place on the island. He was standing almost alone on the little wharf, and his great face beamed with pleasure. . . .

His tall, robust figure, broad shoulders bending a little under the weight of years, his large round face lit up by kindly dark-brown eyes, his cheery smile. . . . He greeted us with great warmth as we landed. He looked into our faces to justify himself in making choice of us among the many whom he might have chosen.

After greeting each student with a handshake, "the great naturalist" led them up the hill to see the new dormitory. It wasn't in the best of shape, construction having run longer than Agassiz had anticipated. The windowpanes hadn't been installed yet, nor had the shingles, and the wall that was to separate the men's from the women's sleeping quarters was, at present, just a flimsy sailcloth hanging from a rafter.

Some of the students were horrified. Frank H. Lattin, a young birdwatcher from Rochester, thought the island's "desolate" location, ramshackle buildings, and inescapable sun made it feel like a kind of hell. "Viewed simply in itself," he writes, "it was a most unattractive spot, and at first I could scarcely persuade myself that I could enjoy my stay here."

But eyes, tricky organs, show different people different things. That same hot earth beckoned to David, its golden sand glittering with mysterious seashells, sponges, seaweed. As the students were beginning to socialize, to flirt, to choose their beds in those long rows of cots, David slipped down to the shore, his fingers grazing salt water for the very first time. He picked up a smooth black stone, then a greenish one, his mind flooding with the panic of his life—"'Is this hornblende?' 'Is this epidote?' 'How do you tell them apart?'"

In time, he was called to join the group up at the barn for a midmorning meal. The sheep had been dragged out only a few days before—four-legged tables dragged in—so the building would have had the smell of hay, of urine, of grass, of life. Spiderwebs and swallow nests still presided from the rafters. This was to be their main classroom for the summer. The students took their places at long tables and chatted away as they dug into their food. There's a chance that during breakfast David glimpsed a flash of auburn hair, belonging to a young botanist from Massachusetts named Susan Bowen. The two would grow close that summer, exploring the shores of Penikese by moonlight, slipping their ankles into the black waves to ignite firework displays of twinkling green bioluminescence.

As the meal concluded, Agassiz rose from his chair to deliver his welcome speech. It was a benediction too beautiful, according to David, to ever re-create. "What Agassiz said that morning can never be said again."

Luckily for us, the famous poet John Greenleaf Whittier was also in attendance that summer and he did not agree with David's assessment. Whittier would later publish a poem called "The Prayer of Agassiz" recounting that very speech. He starts with a bit of scene setting—"On the isle of Penikese / Ringed about by sapphire seas"—and then gets to it, to Agassiz's benediction, the reason collecting mattered.

Said the Master to the youth:
"We have come in search of truth,
Trying with uncertain key
Door by door of mystery:
We are reaching, through His laws,
To the garment-hem of Cause,

Him, the endless, unbegun,
The Unnamable, the One,
Light of all our light, the Source,
Life of life, and Force of force.
As with fingers of the blind,
We are groping here to find
What the hieroglyphics mean
Of the Unseen in the seen.

I've never been great at poetry, but if I'm decoding those capitalizations right then what the taxonomists were searching for as they ogled their precious weeds and rocks and snails was . . .

The Unnamable, the One, the Source, the Force, the Truth, the Unseen . . .

God!

Indeed, in his writings Agassiz is clear: he believes that every single species is a "thought of God," and that the work of taxonomy is to literally "translat[e] into human language . . . the thoughts of the Creator."

Specifically, Agassiz believed that hiding in nature was a divine hierarchy of God's creations that, if gleaned, would provide moral instruction. This idea of a moral code hidden in nature—a hierarchy, a ladder or "gradation" of perfection—has been with us for a long time. Aristotle envisioned a holy ladder—later Latinized to *Scala Naturae*—in which all living organisms could be arranged in a continuum of lowly to divine, with humans at the top, followed by animals, insects, plants, rocks, and so on. And Agassiz believed that by arranging these organisms into their proper order, one could come to discern not just the intent of a holy maker but perhaps even the instructions for how to become better.

Some hierarchies seemed obvious to Agassiz. Take posture, for example. Humans revealed their superiority by how they stood,

"looking heavenward," while fish "[lay] prostrate within the water."
But other hierarchies were more subtle. Look at the parrot, the ostrich, and the songbird. Who among them is the highest on the ladder? If you could crack that, Agassiz figured, then you could learn
which mattered more to God: speech, size, or song. But *how* do
you crack the code? Well, that's where things got fun. That's where
the microscopes and magnifying glasses came in. Using what Agassiz believed were objective measures about organisms, such as "the
complication or simplicity of their structure" or "the character of
their relations to the surrounding world," you could rank organisms in their proper order. Lizards, for example, would score higher
than fish because they "bestow greater care upon their offspring."
Parasites, meanwhile, were clear lowlifes, the lot of them. Just look
at how they earned their living: they mooched and deceived and
freeloaded.

But the most valuable lessons, Agassiz believed, lay hidden
under the skin. At some point during his lecture on Penikese Island, Agassiz would have warned his students about the danger of
outerwear—whatever scales or feathers or quills a creature wore.
This outerwear could be a dangerous distraction, a red herring that
could fool a taxonomist into seeing similarities between creatures
where there were none (hedgehogs and porcupines, for example: on
the outside, they're so similar; on the inside, they're a world apart).
Agassiz explained that the best way to get to God was with a scalpel.
To split the skin and look inside. That was where you would discover the "true relations" of the animals. In their bones, their gristle,
their guts. That was where the divine thoughts lay most exposed.

Take fish, for example. All the fish swimming just outside the
barn at that very moment. Pluck one from the ocean, skin it, and
you would discover a very clear message from God. "We cannot understand the possible degradation and moral wretchedness of Man,
without knowing that his physical nature is rooted in . . . the Fish,"

he writes. To Agassiz, the shockingly similar skeletal plan of fish (their skulls, their vertebrae, their rib-like protrusions) represented a warning to "Man." They were scaly reminders of how far a person could slip if he didn't resist his base urges: "The moral and intellectual gifts that distinguish him from [the fish] are his to use or to abuse. . . . He may sink as low as the lowest of his type, or he may rise to a spiritual height." As Agassiz aged, he eased up just slightly on the idea of the fixity of species in order to leave room for a concept he called "degeneration." He worried that even the highest of creatures could fall from their rungs if they weren't careful, that bad habits could somehow cause a species to physically and cognitively decline.

In this way, Agassiz presented nature as a sacred text. Even the dullest slug or dandelion could offer spiritual and moral guidance to those humans curious enough to look. Take all of those messages in aggregate and you get the intricate, awe-inspiring shape of what he called the divine plan. God's fable-rich explanation of the meaning of it all, not just how all organisms are ranked, but the very road map—written in a convoluted set of morals—to ascension.

"The swallows flew in and out of the building in the soft [summer] air, for they did not know that it was no longer a barn but a temple," writes David Starr Jordan, finally able to use his words again.

Agassiz pressed a nub of white chalk to the blackboard: *A laboratory is a sanctuary where nothing profane should enter*, he wrote. To conclude the lecture, he asked his students to bow their heads in silent prayer to consider the gravity of their summer ahead. According to the poet, even the birds obeyed.

Once the "solemn hush" had passed over the barn, Agassiz warned that those who did not take their time on the island seriously would be sent home.

I imagine David lying awake on his cot that night, staring at the wooden rafter above his head, feeling his world rearranged. Yes, here at last were the words to convince his mother, his classmates, his colleagues, so unmoved by his pursuits. What he was doing with those flowers in his hands was not "pointless" or "wasteful" or "shiftless," it was—as Agassiz himself had defined it—"missionary work of the highest order." It was the work of deciphering God's plan, the meaning of life, and possibly even the path to building a better society. I picture David breathless, ecstatic, eyes on that rafter, realizing that even trying to classify *that* wood—was it pine!? cedar!? oak?—was to do the most purposeful work on the planet. A whole childhood reclaimed. He must have been giddy, heart racing . . . which is perhaps why he didn't hear the rustling of the sheets.

The rustling of women's bodies just a couple of millimeters away through that flimsy sailcloth. The rustling of the auburn-haired woman who was, at that moment, climbing out of her clothes and into her sheets. Skin on sheets making a rustling, which must have agitated some of the male sleepers, because a group of them stuffed a pillow into a blanket and threw the ungainly wad over the (as yet unclassified) rafter. Some of the women screamed and some groaned. And the next morning, according to David:

"Agassiz was distinctly stern. At breakfast he rose and said that six young men (whose names he gave) would leave by the steamer at ten o'clock. Various appeals were now made: 'the women didn't mind it'—'it was only a student prank and had no significance.' But he remained firm. We were there for serious purpose, he said; it was not the place or time for 'pranks.'"

Shortly after those six young men boarded the steamer home in shame, David stepped onto a little schooner rattling with nets and buckets and pride. Having caught Agassiz's eye that first morning as he explored the shoreline inspecting rocks, David was one of the few campers chosen to come along on the first dredging expedition.

"Here I made my first acquaintance with fishes of the sea," David sings, "which were brought up in bewildering variety." He doesn't put names to any of the creatures flopping around in that net, for at that moment they were still mysteries to him, the shimmering and scaly clues beckoning him to a puzzle he would spend the rest of his life trying to solve.

3.

A Godless Interlude

aybe Cape Cod is fertile ground for existential trans-formation. Something about the metals in its sandy soil catalyzing metaphysical shifts—I don't know. All I know is I, too, had my entire worldview rear-ranged when I was visiting its shores. It happened when I was about seven years old, and oddly enough, it was that moment that would pave the way for my obsession with David Starr Jordan, that would make him the kind of person I hoped could save me when my life later unraveled.

It was early morning, early summer. I was on vacation with my family in Wellfleet, Massachusetts, just fifty miles, as the crow flies, from Penikese Island.

I was standing on the deck with my father, trading off a pair of clunky black binoculars, gazing out into a yellow-and-green ex-panse of marsh which rolled out before us. We were trying to get a better look at a white dot we had noticed in the distance. My dad was a tall, mustachioed man, with a mane of jet-black hair in those days, cut-off jean shorts, no shirt, and a fuzzy, friendly belly, nearly always offering a pastel fleck of lint. The rest of the house—my mom, my two older sisters, our cats—was still asleep. Unable to get the lenses to focus properly, I had just handed the binoculars back to my dad. I kept staring at the white dot nestled in the reeds—wondering if it was a swan, a buoy, something more exciting—when for some reason I cannot recall, I asked my dad, "What's the meaning of life?"

Maybe it had been the expansiveness of the marsh, which ended at the ocean, which ended ... I didn't understand where—I pictured an edge, with sailboats tipping off—that made me suddenly wonder what we were all doing here.

My dad paused, raising one black eyebrow behind the binoculars. Then he turned to me grinning and announced, "Nothing!"

It felt like he had been waiting eagerly, for my whole life, for me to finally ask. He informed me that there is no meaning of life. There is no point. There is no God. No one watching you or caring in any way. There is no afterlife. No destiny. No plan. And don't believe anyone who tells you there is. These are all things people dream up to comfort themselves against the scary feeling that none of this matters and you don't matter. But the truth is, none of this matters and you don't matter.

Then he patted me on the head.

I have no idea what my face would have looked like then. Ashen? It was as if a big feather comforter had just been ripped off the world.

Chaos, he informed me, was our only ruler. This massive swirl of dumb forces was what made us, accidentally, and would destroy us, imminently. It cared nothing for us, not our dreams, our intentions, our most virtuous of actions. "Never forget," he said, pointing to the pine-needly soil beneath the deck, "as special as you might *feel*, you are no different than an ant. A bit bigger, maybe, but no more significant"—he paused, consulting the map of hierarchies that existed in his head—"except, do I see you aerating the soil? Do I see you feeding on timber to accelerate the process of decomposition?"

I shrugged.

"I do not. So you are arguably *less* significant to the planet than an ant."

Then, to really drive his point home, he threw his arms wide—I thought maybe this was an invitation for a hug, for him to say *Just kidding, you matter!*—but instead he said, "Okay. Now picture that *this* . . . is all of time." He palpated a vast, invisible time line in front of his chest. "Humans have only been around *this* long!" On the word "this" he theatrically pinched his fingers together. "And we will probably be gone soon! And if you zoom out away from the Earth, well . . ." He clucked. "Then we're *really* nothing. There are planets and beyond them more solar systems . . ."

I'm not sure if he used the exact words, but nearly two decades later when I heard astronomer Neil deGrasse Tyson say his famous line "we are a speck on a speck on a speck," I heard my father's call.

I don't think I had the language as a seven-year-old to put into words the cold feeling that was starting to swirl up my lungs. "So then what's the point of any of this? Why go to school? Why glue macaroni to paper?" But I spent my childhood quietly inspecting my father's behaviors to find out. He's a lively man. A biochemist with shaky hands who studies ions, the particles that carry the electricity that powers all life—heartbeat, lightning, even thought itself. He doesn't use seat belts or return addresses; he swims where it is prohibited, and one day came home declaring he was *done with sleeves*—after they had toppled his test tubes one too many times. In a huff, he had stormed toward his closet with a pair of scissors and then spent the next few years going to work dressed in a way that can best be described as Academic Pirate.

He worships the family dog (who is naughty), refuses to follow recipes, enjoys sampling the taste of his discarded test subjects— frog legs, electric ray organs, though my mom drew the line at mice livers, refusing to let him enter her kitchen to fry up the contents of his greasy paper lunch bag. Once, as he and I were walking into the retirement home where his mother lived, an old woman in a wheelchair accidentally cut us off. *"Slow down!"* my father shouted, and dropped to the floor, writhing and grimacing, as if to insinuate she'd hit him. I was cringing, embarrassed, worried that he would scare this poor woman to literal death. But the light that snapped on in her eye, the smile that unfurled across her face, made me realize she could handle the joke, was hungry for the joke, for being seen as a person who can handle a joke.

You don't matter seems to fuel his every step, his every bite. *So live as you please.* He spent years riding a motorbike, drinks copious amounts of beer, and enters the water, whenever possible, with the belliest of flops. He seems to permit himself just one lie to constrain his otherwise voracious hedonism, to form a kind of moral code. *While other people don't matter, either, treat them like they do.*

He has made my mom coffee almost every morning for half a century. He is devoted to his students—they came to our holiday meals; they sometimes lived in our home. Our kitchen table is etched with thousands of tiny numbers, carved in his shaky hand, a physical record of the countless nights he spent trying to get my sisters and me to comprehend the beauty of math.

What could be a grim reality has instead pumped his life full of vigor. Has made him live big and good. I have strived my whole life to follow in his nihilistic, clown-shoed footsteps. To stare our pointlessness in the face, and waddle along toward happiness because of it.

But I haven't always been so good at it.

You don't matter has often had a different effect on me.

Don't get too squeamish. Camus estimates it's on the mind of a majority of us at any moment. That remedy for pain so enticing that eighteenth-century poet William Cowper smartly termed it the "grand temptation."

For me, it started beckoning when I was in the fifth grade. Around the time my oldest sister got bullied so badly she had to drop out of high school. My sweet sister, with my father's black hair, who wore maroon-rimmed glasses over her dark eyes and shiny braces on her quick-to-smile teeth, who got anxious easily and had trouble understanding social cues, who would flail her hands and pull out her eyelashes and eyebrows when she was stressed. I hated her classmates for not going easier on her, for not cutting her some slack; I hated picturing her walking those hallways and not finding a single pair of eyes offering her refuge. Sometimes it felt nicer not to picture it at all.

I tried to console myself, though, as my dad seemed to do, with Earth's pleasures. Mud pies and fireflies and dams. Oh, how I loved building a good rain-dam. Once dammed a gutter so good, it attracted a duck! But when I got to middle school, the hallways started turning on me, too. "Where's your hammer?" the boys sneered, tugging at the loops in my carpenter pants. They mocked the way I wore my baseball cap, apparently too low. They called me "Jerry" and I didn't understand why. In ninth grade I walked by a group of boys who shouted, "Seven!" It was so clear they were rating girls, ranking us as we walked by. *Seven*, I thought. *Not bad!* Until I found out it was the number of beers they would need to drink to have sex with me. *Seven.* Complete annihilation, then, to be worthy of touch.

I knew a braver girl, a sturdier soul, would laugh back at the boys. I knew how very small my problems were. But I didn't have that thing inside me, whatever it was; when I felt for a backbone all I found was sand.

As I grew older, things only got worse for my sister. She tried going to community college but had to come home after things blew up with her roommate. She earned a degree but had trouble holding jobs. She was too flustered by the cash register, too chatty for the library. She'd come home at night to my mom's worry, my father's disappointment, and bellow behind her bedroom door. I'd picture her changing into elemental form, this tornado of loneliness and tears, and it scared me when she emerged with her face vacuumed of its eyebrows and lashes. Not because it looked alien, but because I knew a sadness that powerful lurked inside me. I preferred to vent it by slicing little nicks into my skin, was all.

My dad seemed weary of both of us, though, impatient for us to cheer up, to get it together, see the good in life and enjoy our time on this rock before it was over. "There is grandeur in this view," scolds a quote from Darwin hanging over my dad's desk at his lab. The words are written in looping brown calligraphy, enclosed in a varnished wooden frame. The quote comes from the last sentence of *On the Origin of Species*. It is Darwin's sweet nothing, his apology for deflowering the world of its God, his promise that there *is* grandeur—if you look hard enough, you'll find it. But sometimes it felt like an accusation. If you can't see it, shame on you.

When my father's mood was off, when he'd had too long a day, too many sips of beer or bourbon, he'd stomp up the stairs to communicate he'd had enough of our shit, breaking his cardinal rule—*other people matter*—by slamming doors or shaking us, a few times slapping my sister so hard it left pink imprints on her skin. My mother would cry under the mounting tension of it all. My middle sister, who had once been the pillar to us all, had understandably begun to extract herself, studying abroad in the deserts of Mali by the time I had landed in the tenth grade.

I remember thinking that there didn't seem to be anywhere good to get to. That the outside world offered only vicious hallways, empty horizons. The inside world, only slamming doors. *I see nothing gleaming,* I wrote in my journal on April 8, 1999. A Sunday. I was newly sixteen. After school the next day, I drove to Walgreens. I made my way to the aisle full of sleeping pills. Some of the boxes were light blue, some of them dark blue, some of them purple. They all twinkled with papery-white stars promising slumber. I slipped a few lavender boxes under my coat. I did not want to cause suspicion.

When I made it home for dinner, everything felt lighter. I waited until the house had gone to sleep. Mom, Dad, curled into each other, great at not fighting when not conscious, Down. Oldest sister, fishlike lids mercifully shut for the evening, Down. Middle sister, sleeping in the home of another, better family somewhere in the middle of Africa, Down. Tiny white dog Charlie, Down. I tiptoed down to the basement. I had not yet read that animals tend to burrow when they are ready to die. I only knew that I was drawn there. I made a ceremony of popping each pill out of its little plastic bubble. One pill per minute. Even atheists like ritual.

I awoke to bright lights. The humiliation of a nurse, my worried mother in a hospital chair, paper sheets beneath my ass, a grid of Styrofoam ceiling tiles as far as the eye could see. I thought about how they looked like Saltines. No, Stoned Wheat Thins. No, Saltines. It was the next day. I was prescribed Paxil, which I was too proud to take. I was banned from attending a school field trip, deemed too much of a risk. The knowledge of what I did snaked odorlessly through the school hallways.

I bought pink lip gloss and smiled extra hard and vowed next time I'd do it right. I began fantasizing about an object. A shiny metal object that would do the job better than pills. By the end of high school, there were days the temptation was so great, I could hardly see past it.

But when I landed in college, I noticed what looked like a gleaming. A goofy, doofy, curly-haired man with broad shoulders brushed by me in the hallway one day. He smelled like cinnamon. He had teddy-brown eyes and performed in the college's improv group. He was the best one by far, made big gestures, made jokes from a place of kindness and whimsy, pulled ripples of laughter out of this cold, hard world. I used to sit in the audience and marvel. He seemed like an impossibility.

It took years. Years of slowly befriending him through mutual friends. Years of calling into his late-night, freestyle-rap radio show, daring my tongue to try . . . to rhyme on the *fly*! I even joined the improv group. And eventually, one night I told him how I felt and instead of flinching away, as I had assumed he would, as the boys in the hallway had made it seem that he would, he kissed me.

After graduating college, we moved in together, to a small one-bedroom apartment in Brooklyn with a red Formica table and a great front stoop. I finagled my way into a job helping produce a radio program all about science and wonder. He was continuing with comedy—stand-up and improv and writing—and working as a yellow-cab driver to support himself. We stayed up late into the night, sipping beers on the stoop, talking about our days, turning awkward moments and missteps into jokes. I felt like I had found the thing I had thought could never exist. Refuge. It smelled like cinnamon and its walls were made of bad puns and cheap rhymes, piling higher and higher against the chill of the world. My head became full of visions for the future. The TV shows we would write, the tree houses we would build, the way the grass would curl between our toes as we chased our kids through the yard. Until, seven years into it, I toppled the whole thing. Late one night on a beach five hundred miles away from him, possessed by moonlight and red wine and the smell of a bonfire, I reached out for the bouncing blond girl I had been trying not to eye all night. She was wet from swimming; she was prickled in goose bumps, hundreds of goose bumps, that I wanted to press flat with my tongue. She smiled as I placed my hand on her waist, as I touched my lips to her neck. The stars wrapped around us. Her steam became mine.

When I told the curly-haired man what I had done, he told me it was over.

But I did not believe him. That I could so quickly ruin this intricate thing we had built together over the years. I begged him to reconsider. I assured him that the girl thing was a blip, a slip-up, that it would never happen again. But he was too angry, too hurt. He did not want to be with the kind of person who could be that reckless. Without him, the world went dark. Our friends knew what I had done and drew away from me. I avoided my family, not wanting to explain what had happened. My work, the science stories I had once chased with such glee, fell flat. Just proof, in various disciplines—chemistry, neurology, entomology—of how bleak and meaningless it all was.

Slowly, the grand temptation began to reappear in my brain. Its barrel beckoning, offering its most glorious gift. Relief.

But from somewhere deep inside me—a backbone, there after all? A deluded corner of my brain?—I came up with an alternate plan. Maybe if I repented hard enough, long enough, the curly-haired man would eventually see how sorry I was and take me back. So, I grabbed my weapon: a pen. I wrote him letter after letter; I waited; I hoped. I lobbed the occasional lame joke his way, our secret birdcall. "Happy Dozen," I emailed on the first day of 2012. No response. I tried not to worry as one year turned to two, two to three. As the silence out my windows whirred louder and louder, the Second Law of Thermodynamics flexing her bottomless tail. I tried to keep faith.

And that, *that* is why David Starr Jordan called out to me. I wondered what it was that allowed him to keep plunging his sewing needle at Chaos, in spite of all the clear warnings that he would never prevail. I wondered if he had stumbled across some trick, some prescription for hope in an uncaring world. And because he was a *scientist*, I held on to the distant possibility that his justification for persistence, whatever it was, fit into my father's worldview. Perhaps he had cracked something essential about how to have hope in a world of no promises, about how to carry forward on the darkest days. About how to have faith without Faith.

But after reading about David's experience on Penikese Island, I was beginning to worry. If God was the light that lit his search through dark times, then he didn't have any more to teach me.

I found my answer when he encountered Darwin. After leaving Penikese Island, David took a job as a science teacher at a small prep school in Appleton, Wisconsin. And the ideas of Darwin, which had been just whispers when David was a little boy, had become a gale-force wind with which every serious scientist needed to contend. *On the Origin of Species* was filled with all kinds of heresies—that all life on Earth evolved from "one primordial form," that humans are still evolving and could, one day, even go extinct. But perhaps the most difficult idea for a taxonomist to accept was that species were not hard, immutable categories in nature. Darwin had observed so much variety in creatures traditionally assumed to be one species that his sense of a hard line between species had slowly begun to dissolve. Even that most sacred line, the supposed inability of different species to create fertile offspring, he realized was bunk. "It cannot be maintained that species when intercrossed are invariably sterile," Darwin writes, "or that sterility is a special endowment and sign of creation." Leading him finally to declare that species—and indeed all those fussy ranks taxonomists believed to be immutable in nature (*genus, family, order, class, etc.*)—were human inventions. Useful but arbitrary lines we draw around an ever-evolving flow of life for our "convenience." *"Natura non facit saltum,"* he writes. *Nature doesn't jump.* Nature has no edges, no hard lines.

Imagine how troubling that would be to you if you were a tax-onomist. Learning that the objects you held in your hands were not puzzle pieces after all, not clues, but products of randomness. They were not pages in a sacred text, not symbols in a holy code, not rungs on a divine ladder. They were snapshots of Chaos in motion. For some, the idea was too maddening. It made the earth feel too bleak, their pursuit too pointless. Louis Agassiz remained adamantly opposed to Darwin until his dying day. He lectured widely on the topic, calling the idea that humans could have evolved from apes "repulsive."

But David Starr Jordan, of a younger generation, with a still-malleable mind, decided eventually, torturously, to break with his "master" on just this count. The closer he looked at nature, the more he realized he couldn't deny Darwin's observations, the reality of the gray area between species; he was beginning, reluctantly, to see it too. He writes, "I went over to the evolutionists with the grace of a cat the boy 'leads' by its tail across the carpet!"

Oh, how this line made me adore David. It made me want to wrap my arms around his chest, plant a kiss on his begrudging cheek, and tell him he was brave, he was good, for heeding the devastating truth of evolution and finding a way to forge on.

It meant, of course, that I could keep using him as my guide. It meant that, perhaps, as brazen as he seemed with his sewing-needle sword, he operated from a place of reason. It meant that denial was not necessarily a path to humiliation. It meant that maybe, just maybe, by following in his overconfident footsteps I would find my way back toward a glimmering refuge after all.

4.

Chasing Tail

t is now that the music montage begins. Cue the jaunty sea shanties and roll back the sleeves of David Starr Jordan and place him on the deck of a giant sailboat alongside a dozen men in bowler caps; arm them with fishing poles, spears, tridents, trawl nets, anything to get fish, fish, more fish out of the water.

After leaving Penikese Island, blessed by Agassiz to take the work of collecting seriously, David set his sights on the water. "[T]he literature of Ichthyology was inexact and incomplete," he writes, "with few comparative studies, so that the field seemed wide open, as indeed it was." As he jumped from teaching job to teaching job at schools all over the Midwest, he set himself the goal of discovering every freshwater fish in North America. For help, he recruited an old taxonomy buddy from his Cornell days, Herbert Copeland. A muscly guy with a bushy brown beard. They moved in together, to a flophouse in Indianapolis, where I picture the bathroom littered with crumpled copies of *Systema Naturae*. Though I've been unable to confirm if they indeed had a bathroom. Plumbing was still spotty in those days, especially in a place as remote as Indiana.

They hit the water, the rivers and lakes, reeling in various specimens, some with whiskers and some with fangs, and most smelling like a mix of pond scum and pickle. Slowly, they began publishing taxonomic studies, illuminating new connections between species, eliminating redundancies—such as *Ictalurus punctatus*, a species of catfish, which David claims "had appeared as a new species twenty-eight times." In time the government took notice of this mop-topped fish addict out west. They asked David to sign on as a sort of mercenary, deploying him over his summer breaks to annihilate more of the American unknown. To Texas he goes, and to Mississippi, Iowa, Georgia, Tennessee, all in search of new fish species on which to plant the US flag of discovery.

In 1880, he was sent (as part of the US Census) to catalogue the fish species that lived along the Pacific coast. He took one of his favorite students with him, a "bright boy" named Charley Gilbert, and, starting in San Diego, they began marching up the coast in search of the country's aquatic residents. David was dazzled by the "oily" "treasures" they pulled from the waves. He writes of the mighty leaping tuna "which reaches a weight of 600 pounds," of the albacore with "long, ribbon-like pectoral fins," of the California flying fish whose "wings" vibrated like "dragonflies" over distances "upward of an eighth of a mile." And slowly, day by day, mile by mile, David and Charley began to catch them. The unknown. Creatures with no names or traces in the scientific record. A small lantern fish with glowing spots, "which had risen from the deeps in a storm." A tiny, rainbow-scaled fish that was found inside the belly of a hake, which was found inside the belly of an albacore. A crimson fish with yellow stripes that they nicknamed "the Spanish flag."

They were at it for months. They celebrated Christmas in San Diego, the Lunar New Year in Santa Barbara. By March, they were scouring the peninsulas of Monterey. As much as David tried to focus on fish, though, it turned out he had a wandering eye for plants. He couldn't resist pointing out the scientific names of the trees they passed, *Cupressus macrocarpa*, *Pinus radiata*. He had also developed a tic of ranking almost every organism they saw. The eulachon: "the most delicious of all fishes." The silver maple: a "second-rate shade tree." The hagfish, the worst of its class for the way it made its living—leaping onto its prey and slurping its insides out: a slime-covered "pirate" with "bad habits."

Ever the disciple of his prophet Louis Agassiz, David examined the organisms he was encountering for moral instruction. He had taken Agassiz's foggy idea of "degeneration," mashed it up with Darwin's theory of evolution, and ran with it. He saw the slimy hagfish as evidence that "bad habits" such as sloth or parasitism could make a species degenerate, devolve, or "change for the worse." In a scientific paper, David proposed that the sea squirt, a sedentary sac of a filter feeder, had once been a higher fish but had "degraded" into its current form due to a combination of "idleness," "inactivity and dependence." He wasn't sure of the exact mechanisms that would cause such a deterioration, but to David, the sea squirt was a clear warning. A cautionary tale in laziness. A literal sad sack.

As David and Charley combed their way up the coast, David studied how the various fishermen caught their prey. The Chinese fishermen in San Diego, who used fine nets to dredge up a wriggling cornucopia of creatures; the Portuguese fishermen of Santa Barbara, who stood on the rocks and plunged three-tined spears into the surf; even the gulls and pelicans, who dove with an enviable precision. He adopted the methods he could and stole when he could not; he plundered Chinese fish markets for creatures unknown to science; he tore into the bellies of birds and sharks in search of creatures that evaded his hand. On that trip alone, David and Charley named over *eighty* new species of fish. Eighty new branches on the tree of life, unveiled. Eighty new species willed into existence by the words rolling off their tongues. *Myctophum crenulare. Sudis ringens. Sebastichthys rubrivinctus.*

Eight months later, David journeyed back to Indiana, this time to Bloomington, where he had finally secured a permanent job as a professor of science at Indiana University. It was also around this time that David accomplished something that had once seemed even harder. He got married! That auburn-haired botanist from Penikese Island. Susan Bowen. He persuaded her to leave her home, in the verdant Berkshire mountains of Massachusetts and join him in Indiana. She moved with some trepidation. Indiana felt like the Wild West; it was undeveloped, far from her family, unruly. But she loved David; she loved the way he loved the world. Shortly after marrying, they had a baby, Edith, and another, Harold, and another, Thora. After only six years of teaching at IU, when David was thirty-four years old, the board of trustees asked him to become president of the institution. He accepted, making him the youngest university president in the entire country. It is right around then that his mustache—two virile tusks unfurling beneath his nostrils—grew in.

This is just conjecture, of course, but how does a man go so quickly from being unnoticed by the human world—mocked for his pursuits and occasionally even abused—to being exalted by it? I picture a meek and murky man, dusty and pale, sliding by unnoticed, slowly filling up with that light, that air, that radiant matter, whatever it is, of Purpose.

It makes a difference in a life.

His hunt, by the way, though extinguished of its God by Darwin, David considered no less noble. As David saw it, he was still on the hunt for the shape of the ladder that revealed how all creatures and plants were ordered—only now he believed its arrangement had been forged by time, not God. But the secrets it had to tell were no less crucial, no less revealing. By looking very closely at fish anatomy, he told himself, he was discovering our true creation story, what experiments in life it took to make humans. And he was uncovering the clues—written in the accidental missteps and successes of other creatures—that could potentially help our kind advance even further. It was Agassiz's same mission, but without a creator at the helm.

And David was making headway. His burly, bespectacled crew of taxonomists were discovering fish faster than they could name them. They were preserving them in jars of ethanol and stacking them on shelves inside David's secluded lab on the top floor of the science building. Thousands of mysterious creatures being piled higher and higher, awaiting their sacred naming ceremony.

Until late one night in July of 1883, the universe cracked her knuckles—those tiny pockets of ions hiding in the air—and released a lightning bolt that hit a telephone wire and threw sparks into the office below David's lab. A few sheets of paper caught fire. Then more sheets. Then the walls. Until eventually the flames were licking their way toward the shelves holding David's precious jars. Ethanol, though fabulous at stalling the universe's attempts at decay, is friend to fire. The jars would have exploded like tiny bombs. Fish were vaporized. Unidentified creatures were incinerated, possibly never to be found again. Every last specimen was destroyed. And that wasn't all. For years, David had been working on a secret document, a treasure map of sorts, revealing never-before-seen branches of the tree of life. A huge and chandeliering chart made up of frenetic lines declaring insight, declaring evolutionary connections—completely torched. The reporter charged with assessing the damage could barely contain his grief. "[T]he flames of an hour had near undone his life work," he writes in the *Bloomington Telephone*.

But David Starr Jordan refused to be stalled by the catastrophe. He dusted up the ashes, and headed right back out to the nation's bodies of water to retrieve what he had lost. He did not linger on how much time he'd wasted; he did not consider the seeming futility of what he was trying to do—to make order in a world ruled by Chaos. He claimed to have learned only one lesson from the whole ordeal. What was it? To stay humble? To set more reasonable goals than, say, cataloguing every freshwater fish of North America? "To publish at once," he writes. Oh, to push harder.

He had a similar reaction when tragedy struck his personal life. One November day, just two years later, his wife, Susan, came down with a cough. Her auburn hair went damp with the sweat from a fever. Days later, she was dead. Killed, as their daughter Edith explains, by a bout of pneumonia the "rural town doctors were unable to cure."

Again, David moved quickly. He ordered an extravagant arrangement of white chrysanthemums to drape over Susan's coffin. He delivered an eloquent eulogy, in which he reminisced about their shared loved of taxonomy, their nighttime walks on the beach at Penikese, where the "water shone as bright as stars on account of the minute animal life which it contained." Perhaps he even told himself Susan would have wished it this way, her death an unfortunate casualty on their worthy mission of order.

And then, as he had with the fish, he headed right back out to the nation's wilds, to retrieve what he had lost. Less than two years after Susan's death, he had caught himself a new wife. A college sophomore named Jessie Knight, who was, in many ways, an upgrade for David. Where Susan had bemoaned David's traveling, writing that she was lonely, that she hated how much time he spent away from the family, Jessie simply asked to come with. She was youthful, energetic, with dark eyes that mesmerized David. When he looked into them, "black as the obsidian stone," he writes, he searched for a distant figure roaming through her genetic past—a "rover from . . . Spain?" A practitioner of "sorcery"? "Some Doña Plácida?" Heredity had become the lens through which he saw the world; it was exactly what he was trying to uncover in his fish—how traits are passed down, how certain physical attributes could reveal clues about evolutionary relationships—and he couldn't seem to shake the impulse when he turned to humans.

Once an eighteen-year-old Jessie landed in Bloomington, she sent David's two eldest children away to boarding school—an act that Edith, ten years old at the time, said forever steeled her against her stepmother. "I knew then that I would never call her mother," she writes, in a handwritten remembrance, toward the end of her life. The baby of the family, Thora, was not to be Jessie's concern; she had passed away of an unnamed illness shortly after her mother's death.

With a newly childless home, Jessie was free to join David on his collecting expeditions. In pictures, she sports a bonnet, spectacles, a coy smile. In David's descriptions, she can be found reclining under a tree, reading a book, while David fishes nearby. He confesses in his memoir, "I may only hint at what her companionship has meant to me."

Of his speedy recoveries from both the lightning and Susan's death, David explains that somewhere along the way he had developed what he calls a "shield of optimism." He guesses that his height may have had something to do with it; fully grown, he was six foot two, gargantuan in those days, when the average height for an American man was about five foot six. Whatever the reason, he said that friends would comment on it, this shield, how he seemed unfazed by setbacks. A colleague of his once quipped that no matter how bad the day, David could always be found "humming a tune adown the arcade."

"I never worry over a mischance, once it is past," David explains. A shrug in his tone.

In time, a wealthy California couple heard about David Starr Jordan—this cheerful, swashbuckling giant with hundreds of notches of scientific discovery on his belt. Their names were Leland

and Jane Stanford, and one day in 1890, they traveled all the way to Bloomington to ask if he would become the first president of their little academic experiment in the farmlands of Palo Alto. David was intrigued by the offer, the generous salary, the glorious weather, the promise of reuniting with those *oily treasures* of the Pacific Ocean. His only hesitation was the Stanfords themselves. Leland Stanford was a Republican senator who was widely considered a robber baron. His wife, Jane, had little formal education and was fond of visiting mediums to try to reach their deceased son. David worried that if he accepted, he would feel like a kept man, a pawn, controlled by the whims of two people whom he considered his moral and intellectual inferiors. But ... that weather ... that salary. In 1891, he was sworn in as the founding president of Stanford University. He had just turned forty years old.

Once David reached Palo Alto, it turned out it was not difficult at all to persuade the Stanfords to let him spend their questionably earned fortune however he pleased. He immediately built a shiny new marine research facility on the tip of the Monterey Peninsula, the Hopkins Seaside Laboratory, modeled after Agassiz's summer camp on Penikese, where direct observation would reign. There were more windows than walls in that thing; the ocean was piped straight into the classroom. He hired a bunch of his friends and former students to stock the Stanford science departments. Charley Gilbert, that "bright boy" turned "brilliant" taxonomist: David appointed him head of the zoology department. David also shipped out the majority of his new fish collection—jars rattling, fish eyes rolling, as the train chugged by snow-capped mountains—and designated one of the most formidable buildings on Stanford's campus to house it when it arrived. A sturdy sandstone behemoth with sweeping archways and a fireproof roof of festive clay tiles. Out front, a marble statue was hoisted over the main entryway. A famous naturalist with bushy mutton chops, a barrel chest, clutching a book in his hand. Can you guess who it was?

Louis Agassiz, of course.

The statue had actually been the Stanfords' idea—they had long admired Agassiz's teaching philosophies—but David was overjoyed. It didn't seem to bother him that by the time the statue was commissioned, Agassiz's image was anything but pure. Not only had Agassiz failed to accept the theory of evolution (the mark of a scientific fool by that point), but his faith in a natural hierarchy had empowered him to advance one of the most hateful and destructive fallacies in scientific history. Till his dying day, Agassiz was one of the country's loudest proponents of the idea of polygenism—the belief that races are different species, and that black people, in particular, were subhuman. He lectured widely and forcefully on the topic. When consulted by the Lincoln administration during the Civil War, for example, he had given his opinion that blacks, if freed, should be segregated from whites, because they would never be able to live peacefully among them. Citing bunk measures and imaginary ranks, Agassiz asserted that black people were biologically "unfit" for civilization. It wasn't their fault, he said, it was simply a matter of science: they were too "childlike" and "sensuous" and "playful" by nature. Too low on that immutable ladder of life.

None of this seemed to worry David, though. He cheered the hoisting of the statue over the entrance to his scientific "sanctuary." He said he forgave Agassiz for rejecting Darwin, because, as David justified it, "[Agassiz] taught us to think for ourselves." He did not seem concerned that his own mind might have been infected by the idea that certain humans were biologically inferior. David, taking after his brother, Rufus, had long identified as an abolitionist; perhaps he figured that alone would keep him immune.

✶ ★ ✳

Just a short distance from the science building, David and Jessie moved into a small stone cottage that they took to calling Escondite, Spanish for "hiding place." It was nestled inside a dense grove of eucalyptus trees, and there, amidst twinkling mists of pine and mint, they began constructing their own personal Garden of Eden. David planted fig trees and lemon trees, firethorn bushes and cacti, apple trees and poppies and squashes and a mix of tropical flowers, "which ultimately grew into a crowded, incongruous, but delightful jungle" containing specimens from "nearly every quarter of the globe." He introduced a monkey named Bob, two parrots (one spoke Spanish; the other, Latin), a cluster of mewling kittens, and a jowly Great Dane. He claimed that when conditions were right, when the monkey was calm and handed the reins just so, it would ride the dog around like a horse. In time, David and Jessie moved into a bigger home and added two humans to their psychedelic menagerie: Knight and Barbara.

David was enthralled with Barbara. She came out with Jessie's obsidian eyes, and he took to calling her his "black-eyed Puritan," and asking her in verse form, "Come to me, and tell me true / Whence those black eyes came to you." As she grew up, David was delighted to discover that she shared his passion for taxonomy. They would take long walks around the campus, searching for bugs or birds or flowers to classify. One day, when she was just seven years old, Barbara pointed at a black bird and "spontaneous[ly]" classified it as a waxwing. David saw this as proof that there must be a genetic component to taxonomy skills and urged future scientists to study the heredity of the taxonomic mind (never mind all the taxonomy books on the shelves, the obvious observation that an interest in taxonomy would have been a quick way to her father's heart). In his memoir, David commits the cardinal sin of parenting by deeming

Barbara "the sweetest, wisest, comeliest, and most lovable" of all his children.

Unhindered by financial constraints, at Stanford David commissioned fish-collecting expeditions to the places he had only been able to dream of, and map, as a boy. To Samoa he went, and to Russia, Cuba, Hawaii, Albania, Japan, Korea, Mexico, Switzerland, Greece, and beyond.

Subheadings in his memoir for this era include: "I touch bottom!" "I attend a *luau*!" (Exclamations added for emphasis but seem potent in spirit.) And: "Japanese Humor," "Moon fête," "A rattler overboard," "Back to Pago Pago," "Sharks and sharks," "Cussing on the up grades," "The lady repents," and "The 'squeeze.'" If you flip to a section titled "'Miss Jessie' meets a griffin," you'll discover that on their trip to Samoa, Jessie did *not*, in fact, encounter the eagle-headed lion of Greek mythology, but a large bat, which David identifies as a "flying fox."

Photographs from these trips show gaggles of men in bowler hats crowded into rowboats, or puffing out their chests in front of beached whales, wrecked ships, Alpine cliffs. There are pictures of flying fish, breaching whales, erupting volcanoes. There's a breathless account of Charley Gilbert getting struck by a falling boulder as they climbed the Matterhorn. Charley survived, but just barely; he suffered a serious head wound and had to be carried down the mountain by a guide. It is one of the few times David confesses to feeling "fright" in his entire life. As they explore new waters, David and his men bring back strange fishes by the barrelful; marbled eels and electric rays and lungfish and tuskfish and lantern fish and seahorses and hammerheads and flounders, pickling in ethanol. The men get increasingly creative in their naming. They name ugly fishes after their enemies, pretty fishes after friends. They are not shy to pay homage to their leader. A little flame of a fish plucked from Hawaiian waters gets the name Jordan's wrasse, *Cirrhilabrus jordani.* There is Jordan's snapper. Jordan's grouper. Jordan's sole. *Lutjanus jordani. Mycteroperca jordani. Eopsetta jordani.* They are nearing a thousand. A thousand new species that in all the millennia of human history only David and his men have been able to find.

The only mark on David's dream life was turning out to be the woman who was making it all possible. Jane Stanford. Just a year into David's presidency, Leland Stanford had died and left Jane in charge of affairs. And it was turning out that Jane was not such a fan of the swashbuckling giant after all. She expressed concern about the amount of time and money David was devoting to fish. She wanted the university to expand in other directions, such as, say . . . the scientific study of spiritualism! There were X-rays in the air— X-rays and electrons and radioactivity all being discovered during those final years of the nineteenth century—and Jane was hopeful that some of these technologies might lead to breakthroughs in contacting the dead.

David found the notion absurd. One of his favorite pastimes was debunking mediums; he would attend séances in San Francisco just to figure out how the "frauds" worked, pointing out their fake beards, their hidden wires, magnets, horns, balloon gas, and other paraphernalia that made the "sleight-of-hand performances" possible. There was no way he was going to take Jane's request seriously. Instead, he began publishing thinly veiled rebukes of people who believed in such notions. In *Science*, in *Popular Science*, he published satires about charlatans who claimed to have discovered "the soul of an atom" or "astral doubles." He even came up with a name for the field: *sciosophy.* The unfortunate fusion of science with philosophy. "Instruments of precision, logic, mathematics, the telescope, the microscope and the scalpel are not needed in sciosophy," he jabbed, in a piece published in *Science*, "because life is short and humanity demands quick returns."

His bone to pick in the end, however, was not with the hucksters making a buck off easy targets but with the easy targets themselves. Such loose thinking, such "trying to believe what we know is not true," he wrote, led to a "vast amount of suffering in our society." A brain that hopeful, that susceptible to flights of fancy, in other words, could become an instrument of evil.

It's unclear if Jane Stanford ever read any of these essays, if they were ever "accidentally" slid across her desk, or if it simply felt good to let off a little steam.

Whatever the case, David likely began to find Jane's silhouette—that black Victorian dress and floral hat sliding across campus—an unwelcome sight. Every time she bumped into him, it seemed, she had a new gripe about his leadership. She raised concerns over David's hiring practices, accused him of nepotism. She called the men in his science departments his "pets."

But to nurse these criticisms, these insults, these painful yanks on his leash, there was always the relief of fish. That wide and watery world offering infinite comfort, better comfort, he was sure, than any booze or drug could provide. With each new fish, each new catch, each new name placed on a formerly unknown piece of the universe, came that impossibly intoxicating feeling. That sweet *honey* on the tongue. That hit of *fantasized omnipotence*. That lovely sensation of order. What a salve, a name.

5.

Genesis in a Jar

here's an idea in philosophy that certain things don't exist until they get a name. Abstract things like *justice, nostalgia, infinity, love,* or *sin.* The thinking goes that these concepts do not sit out there on some ethereal plane waiting to be discovered by humans but instead snap into being when someone invents a name for them. The moment the name is uttered, the concept becomes "real," in the sense that it can affect reality. We can declare *war, truce, bankruptcy, love, innocence,* or *guilt,* and in so doing, change the course of people's lives. The name itself is a thing of great power, then, the vessel that drags the idea from the imaginary to the earthly realm. Before the word, however, the thinking goes, the concept is largely inert.

There are plenty of naysayers. Who roll their eyes and point to math. Do numbers not exist without our names for them? Show me a circle without a pi inside.

But plenty of philosophers take it even further. Trenton Merricks, for example—a philosopher at the University of Virginia—is so dubious about the existence of the concepts around us that he doesn't even think something as seemingly concrete as a chair exists. He agrees that he is sitting on particles, yes, but do those particles constitute "a chair"? He doesn't think so.

His kids have grown up saddled with this knowledge. That he does not believe in chairs or gloves or most human-named categories of objects on Earth. On a school field trip to an apple orchard, his daughter stepped up to him and demanded he answer, in front of parents and schoolkids alike, if he thought the hay cart in which they were all riding existed. He looked around sheepishly, tried to backpedal it, but when she finally pushed him to answer "True or false: this hay cart exists," he looked down and replied, "False."

He said he knows how he sounds; if you were to meet him on an airplane, he wouldn't tell you what he studies: "I try to avoid leading with the thing that's easiest to make fun of. But I actually think the view's not crazy." His point is simply that the human mind is not always so good at carving up its world, that the names we place on things often turn out to be wrong. Were "slaves" subhuman creatures, unworthy of freedom? Were "witches" deserving of the stake? His chair example is intended in the same spirit: a reminder to stay humble, to stay wary of what we believe, about even the most basic things in our lives. "I think you have to think that if you want to make progress."

I got it. I really sort of got it. It felt important as I sat there with him in his office—which did not necessarily exist. But as I walked back out onto campus, orange leaves twirling down so beautifully before me, the ideas seemed to evaporate in the wind. Of course chairs exist. And trees. And leaves. And Love!

There are things in this world that are real. That do not need our words to be real.

What does a fish care if some taxonomist, walking a few feet above him, happens to label him a "fish." With or without his name, he is still a fish. . . .

Right?

Right?

I'll get there.

What's for certain is that taxonomists, also, get a little woo-

woo about the whole naming thing. The very first time a species is named, the specimen is placed in a very special jar, where it receives a very special honor. It is marked in the official scientific ledger as the sole maker of the species. In taxonomic lingo, any specimen is called a "type," and, happily, this holy type happens to be called a "holotype."

And like any sacred relic, these holotypes are stored in safe places—museums or academic institutions all over the world. The very first *Lycaeides idas longinus* butterfly, for example, is stored in Harvard's Museum of Comparative Zoology; the first starfish of the now-extinct *Marocaster coronatus* species, a mosaicked little pendant of a creature, is kept inside the Muséum de Toulouse. They are often kept in private back rooms, but if you ask real nice, with proper reverence for what you seek, you can sometimes be taken to see these things, and stand before them breathless, encountering, in some real way, Genesis in a Jar.

One important rule about holotypes. If one is ever lost, you cannot simply swap a new specimen into the holy jar. No, that loss is honored, mourned, marked. The species line is forever tarnished, left without its maker. A new specimen will be chosen to serve as the physical representative of the species, but it is demoted to the lowly rank of "neotype."

Neotype: a specimen later selected to serve as the representative specimen for a species when the original holotype has been lost or destroyed.

Even scientists like ritual.

There is a clicking in the hallway. Of footsteps on linoleum. I am on my way to behold the only fish in the entire sea that David Starr Jordan named after himself.

The precious holotype is housed behind guarded gates inside our national collection—the Smithsonian's massive annex specimen library some twenty miles outside the capital.

The building is cold. Climate-controlled. Mostly windowless. There is a sharp, ever-present smell of ethanol. Pine mixed with Scotch tape.

The clicking is made up of six feet. I am being escorted by two government taxonomists, with badges strung around their necks.

We walk past a roomful of ungulates, hooves and antlers sticking out of drawers, past the hall of reptiles, some with tails the length of a carpet, toward the bowely section of the building that houses the fish. We are greeted by a locked door. Covertly, one of the taxonomists punches in a key code and whirls us into a room that looks like a library, only instead of books on the shelves, there are jars. Big jars. Little jars. Each with at least one bloated corpse bobbing in yellowing liquid. A giant eel is accordioned into a glass barrel like a gargantuan piece of ribbon candy. A small jar full of minnows looks like a jar of capers. There are fish that look like scorpions, like Koosh balls, like old men, like tinfoil oragami. So odd to think this is what we came from. So odd to think that in embryonic form, we are nearly identical.

Finally, we arrive at the holotype I have come to see. Specimen #51444. *Agonomalus jordani.* It was discovered by David Starr Jordan off the coast of Japan and given its name in 1904. It is a tiny black dragon at the bottom of a mason jar.

One of the scientists unscrews the top, sticks a pair of metal tongs down into the jar, clamps hold of the dragon, and lifts it into the air. She holds it there for a moment, its black scales gleaming under the bright lights, the ethanol dripping onto the linoleum tiles; then she places it into the palm of my hand.

I didn't imagine I'd be allowed to touch something so holy. The creature itself is sharp. It is covered in spines. Spines that could draw blood if you press hard enough, but I resist the urge. I touch the knot of thread that ties its name to the skin, burly, defiant, still there over a century later. I wonder if David's own fingers tied it. The creature's snout is barbed. Its body twirls around itself like a spiral staircase. Its fins look like dragon wings, serrated and sharp. Poacher fish, the family to which the *Agonomalus jordani* belongs, are known for being extraordinary hunters. They camouflage themselves in seaweed to blend in with the gunky outcroppings where they stalk their prey—little crabs and shrimp. Then they use their massive pectoral fins, those dragon wings, to strike at incredible speeds. The unsuspecting crustaceans rarely know what hit them before it's too late.

An eerie quiet falls over me. I wonder why, of all the thousands of fish David encountered, this was the one he chose to name after himself. It's breathtaking, absolutely, but frightening, too, in the way of an M. C. Escher drawing. Something about its form doesn't seem to quite obey the laws of physics. But when you trace your finger along its contours, searching for where the breakdown in geometry occurs, you come up empty. Indeed, its genus name, *Agonomalus*, comes from the Greek for "no corners." *A* = without + *gonias* = angle, corner. Taxonomists from long ago had also noticed how its kind seems to defy the laws of physics. *Agonomalus jordani*. Jordan of the No Corners. Like a Möbius strip, two sides, but one, somehow. The boundary between them an unfindable thing.

Why was this the creature David felt reflected him? Was there some sort of confession in the choice? Of some dark side lurking beneath the friendly man so capable of winning hearts, jobs, awards? I didn't know.

I knew only that the more fish David brought in, the more brutally the universe seemed to strike back.

It wasn't just his wife Susan and his baby Thora that the universe stole as he battled Chaos. There was also his good friend Herbert Copeland. That bearded fisherman whom David recruited to help discover new freshwater fish in North America. One day while out collecting on Indiana's White River, Herbert toppled overboard and froze to death. "Thus out of my life passed my most intimate early friend, and one of the brightest minds with which I was ever associated," writes David. And it didn't stop there; shortly after Herbert died, one of David's favorite students, Charles McKay, went missing while searching for new fish in Alaska. After that, it was his student Charles H. Bollman, who contracted malaria while collecting in the Okefenokee Swamp of southern Georgia and died a rapid death.

But did these deaths scare David back from the pursuit of order for even a second? Not at all. In his signature way, when Chaos struck out, he doubled down, hitting back harder. He began inventing more aggressive techniques for capturing fish. Blowing them out of the water with dynamite, hammering them out of coral, and perhaps most ingenious, for the "myriads of little fishes" that hid inside the tiny cracks in tide pools: poison. David began sprinkling a few pinches of poison into tide pools and watching as, *presto*, a cornucopia of dead sculpins and sea stars and gobies came bobbing to the surface.

Again, he was discovering new species faster than he could name them. Strange corpses were piling higher and higher inside his sandstone temple of a lab at Stanford. He was beginning to feel a leavening in his chest, a sweetness, that feeling of orderliness, of understanding, of agency, regained.

And there sat the world, quietly, patiently, the size of the world, ready to prove him wrong.

In the year 1900, it would set its sights on Barbara. His favorite child. The lover of taxonomy with black eyes, with whom he used to wander the grounds of Escondite, monkey riding the dog by their side, searching for birds and plants to identify, making up stories, at peace enough, even, to debate the existential nature of things. "Walking once with her in the garden," he reminisces, "I repeated Riley's poem, 'The Gobelins will get you if you don't watch out.' 'But there isn't any such thing as a goblin, there never was and never is going to be such a thing,' said she. 'Maybe,' I remarked, reminiscent of [philosopher George] Berkeley's idealism, 'there isn't any such thing as anything.' 'Oh, yes, there is,' she answered, 'there is such a thing as anything,' and, looking around for an unquestioned reality, added triumphantly, 'There is such a thing as a *squash*.'"

One day, while David was off collecting fish in Japan, a nine-year-old Barbara came down with scarlet fever. He rushed home to be by her side but was informed as he landed at the San Francisco docks that he was too late. David calls it "the most cruel personal calamity we have ever experienced," and the "most crushing blow that ever befell my wife or me; the brightest light had gone out of our lives. As I write today after twenty years, the wound seems as deep as yesterday."

The only thing that could offer him some meager relief, a feeble sense of purpose, of distraction? His fish. He went back to the water, back to sea, in search of more, more.

When people have this feeling of personal inefficiency, compulsive collecting helps them in feeling better.

Unfortunately for David, however, Chaos was not the only adversary he had to worry about. As David ticked into his late forties, as his mustache sprouted its first strands of white, Jane Stanford, in her long black dress, continued to nag at David, to question his every move, to yank him away from his fish. Her concerns about his leadership—her charges of nepotism, of extravagant spending—

grew to the point where she appointed a spy to keep tabs on him. The spy was a bearded, bald-headed professor in the German department named Julius Goebel. Jane instructed Goebel to take notes on David's activities and report anything concerning back to her.

And just a few years after Barbara's death, the spy caught David doing something that didn't look great. It had been Charley Gilbert's fault. Good old Charley Gilbert. His student turned traveling companion turned chair of Stanford's zoology department. Charley, long-healed from his hiking accident, long-married, had begun an affair with a young Stanford woman. He and the woman were discovered one day by a librarian, who came to David demanding that Charley be fired for such impropriety. But David did not want to lose Charley from his ranks—that "brilliant" taxonomic mind!—so David, thinking on his feet, threatened the librarian with "incarceration in the insane asylum for sexual perversity" (often code for homosexuality) if he breathed a word of it to anyone else.

That succeeded in shutting the librarian up—he quit Stanford, left town. But somehow Jane's spy got wind of the whole saga, and typed it up in a formal letter to Jane. In it, Goebel accused David of "whitewashing" a sex scandal to protect a friend, and he claimed that this was far from a lone incident. According to the spy, David ran the university like a "gang," with faculty members afraid of disagreeing with him for fear of "risking their heads." Goebel ended his letter with a direct plea to Jane: "Conditions like these are, as you said yourself, a disgrace to scholarship and they must be remedied at once, if your plans of a great University are to be carried out at all."

Then Jane, this woman David considered his moral and intellectual inferior, who had built her empire on seedy money, who was so susceptible to suggestion she believed that *sciosophy* could reach her dead son—she dared to write via signed letter to the senior trustee that David's moral shortcomings had "been painfully evident to me for a long time." By the end of 1904, according to scholar Luther

Spoehr, "rumors abounded that Mrs. Stanford planned to replace Jordan."

Which made it fortuitous that one night in early 1905, Jane died unexpectedly while traveling in Hawaii. It appeared the universe had finally cut David a break.

After Jane's death, David fired the spy from Stanford. Then, with no one on his back to protest, he planned another extended tour of Europe. He brought Jessie. They meandered through the cathedrals of London, the lavender fields of France, the verdant vistas of the Swiss Alps. In Germany, they hopped aboard a riverboat and took a multiday trip down the Moselle, intermittently admiring and tasting the spread of aquatic creatures nipping at their wake.

In time, they returned home to California, to no daughter but a young son, Eric, conceived a couple of years after Barbara's death. By the fall of 1905, he was two years old. And David vowed to keep him safe. He got back to work, walking under the statue of his prophet each morning, to perform what he saw as "missionary work of the highest order." With a scalpel in his hand, he'd remove an unknown specimen from its jar, stare at it under bright lights, prodding its teeth, its fins, its scales, and finally slicing its skin to discover its secrets. He was looking for clues in its bones and organs about which creature begot which, about the direction life flowed, about the experiments it took to make humans, and maybe even tricks to improve them. How was it, exactly, that the lantern fish glowed? That the sea star regenerated its limbs? That the flying fish flew? What adaptations could be borrowed to reduce human suffering, to take humanity to new heights?

He'd examine each creature's guts, its nerves and ligaments, its air bladders and gallbladders and bones and eyeballs; he'd stare deep into its coiled brain for hours, for weeks, sometimes for years, until he was sure he understood what lay before him. Then, cracking his knuckles, perhaps, or removing a crick from his neck, he would inhale some of Earth's good air, and exhale, for the first time ever, its name. *Agonomalus jordani.* And just like that, a new species would wake into being.

To plant his flag on the unknown, he would punch the holy name into a tin tag, drop the tag into the jar alongside the specimen, and seal the lid. Another corner of the universe captured. He displayed his discoveries like trophies, names facing outward as though to taunt the world, stacking them higher and higher, until the amount of Chaos he had brought into order towered nearly two stories high.

6.

Smash

nd then. At 5:12 a.m. on April 18, 1906, Earth shrugged. "In less than a minute . . . the mountains had been torn open to a depth of no one knows how many miles, and then clapped together again as if nothing had happened!" That is David Starr Jordan trying to make geological sense of one of the most traumatic moments of his life: the San Francisco earthquake of 1906. An estimated 7.9 on the Richter scale. In just forty-seven seconds, huge portions of the city collapsed. In the crumbling and subsequent explosions and fires, over three thousand people were killed.

But David didn't know any of this as he awoke to find his body being tossed about "as a rat might be shaken by a dog." He sprinted for Eric's room, refusing to let him go the way of Barbara, to let the universe get him, too. As he raced down the hallway, he called to his grown son, Knight, by then eighteen years old, who had been sleeping on the roof that night. An eerie and ominous score rang out from the parlor below—the piano being played by the ceiling falling discordantly onto the keys. David found little Eric safe in his bed, took him into his arms, and rushed to the stairway, which "jumped about in the most violent fashion, so that it was by no means easy . . . to go down."

Eventually David, Jessie, and Eric made it outside, where an odd calm awaited them. The birds, he wrote, "had already resumed their

singing, and the face of Nature, brazen with spring, seemed absolutely to deny the catastrophe."

A few moments later, Knight stumbled out to report that the
whole university had "gone bum." "Clinging to a wabbling balus-
trade," he'd watched the castles of the sandstone kingdom fall like
dominoes; he described the "fall of the beautiful Church tower with
its graceful flying buttresses, the collapse of the Memorial Arch,
the stones of which flew in every direction 'like water from a fountain,' and the crumbling of the great unfinished library and almost-
completed gymnasium, which (having no adequate support of steel)
went down like a house of cards."

Realizing that he was not just a man, still alive on Earth, but also
the ruler of this crumbled kingdom, David hurried as quickly as he
could to the campus.

It was not even 6:00 a.m. yet. Students were shaken out of their
dorms, like ants from a picnic basket, scattered all over the lawn, dis-
oriented and seeking in one another's eyes or shoulders the confirma-
tion of some stability left on Earth. He ran past them. Past heaps of
fallen buttresses, past the rubble of the welcome arch, past—he would
later learn—dead bodies, crushed by fallen metal and stone. He ran
past the screams of steam blowing out through uprooted water pipes,
past sparking electrical wires, straight to his temple of fish.

"Full of apprehension," he writes, he walked through the door.

What words go here?

Imagine seeing thirty years of your life undone in one instant.
Imagine whatever it is you do all day, whatever it is you care about,
whatever you foolishly pick and prod at each day, hoping, against all
signs that suggest otherwise, that it matters. Imagine finding all the
progress you have made on that endeavor smashed and eviscerated
at your feet.

Those words go here.

Fish were everywhere. Glass was strewn all over the floor. Flounders bashed further flat by fallen stone. Eels severed by shelves. Blowfish popped by shards of glass. There was a pungent smell of ethanol and corpse. But far worse than any of the carnal damage was the existential. For many of those specimens left intact, hundreds of them, nearly a thousand, their holy name tags had scattered all over the laboratory floor. In those forty-seven seconds, Genesis had been reversed: his meticulously named fish had become an amorphous unknown again.

And as if that weren't enough, when David stumbled back outside to seek guidance from his prophet, he saw it.

The quake had thrown the statue of Louis Agassiz headfirst into the concrete. A ludicrous sight. A punch line. His feet pointing to the sky, his little marble hand still clutching its scientific book—this text he believed would chart the course to order, having led him finally to its inevitable end, his head buried in the (for what is concrete, but water mixed with . . .) sand.

If I were the director of this particular play, I'd tell the set designers to dial it back a notch. But there you go, this is what the universe gave us. To me, there is no clearer message: Chaos reigns.

It is now that I would have given up. My prophet desecrated, my dream shattered, decades of persistence proved futile, I would have headed for the basement to give in, at long last, to the *great temptation.*

So what does David do?

What does our careful man of science, who wants above all else to see the world for what it is, do? Does he hear what seems to be the obvious message of the earthquake? That entropy is the way of the world and no human can ever stop it?

Nope. This is when the bastard, the wonderful bastard, takes out his sewing needle and plunges it straight into our ruler's throat.

Where did the idea come from? The idea to stitch a name directly to flesh? Did it rise from somewhere deep within David, the needle surfacing from his boyhood memories of sewing rags into rugs? Did someone else suggest it? A colleague? A student? His wife?

I don't know. Unfortunately, I haven't been able to find the genesis story of the stitching technique. He was likely not the first taxonomist to think of sewing a label directly to a specimen. All we know is that he was the one who oversaw the procedural change in his own collection, and that his desperation to restore order to his fish is evident in the paper trail of requests he issues for help. He asks for "the services of a carpenter . . . to put small slats along the front of the shelves containing bottles of specimens," for "alcohol [to preserve the fish specimens]," for a "steel wall and floor brace[s]."

The responses came back too slowly, though. The alcohol failed to arrive. The fish were lying there, vulnerable to the elements, beginning to desiccate and decay. So David turned to his men, his disciples on the mission of order, and, unable to think of anything else, commanded they arm themselves with hoses.

"The wreckage lay on the floor, kept wet with water from hoses manned day and night by Professors Snyder and Starks," comes one of the most beautiful images I have ever encountered, from one of the least likely of sources: *A Catalogue of the Type Specimens of Recent Fishes in the Natural History Museum of Stanford University*, by J. Böhlke, *The Stanford Ichthyological Bulletin*, Volume 5.

Hoses manned day and night.

Day and night.

The sun rose and fell, rose and fell, and two of David's colleagues stood in galoshes, hoses aimed at a pile of flesh. Is this perhaps a glimpse of the true bones of persistence? Cold and uncertainty splashing in their faces, their prophet upturned outside their window, dust looming in the air, not sure how they'd ever put the mess back together, but at least for now keeping things wet. David ran around attending to worried parents, traumatized students, university accountants with their pencils aghast, all the while sending frantic messages to farflung colleagues to send ethanol. *Day and night.* He allowed the students to sleep outside on the lawn, as many of them were now terrified of ceilings, of shelter. *Day and night.* Friends and colleagues were lowered into the earth. *Dust to Dust.* The dust temporarily settling, as though in a temporary truce, then rising, swirling and rushing David's laboratory windows, bearing mites and putrescine and bacteria, threatening to begin its irreversible process of decay.

The men watered and watered and watered.

Maybe such unruly persistence is beautiful.

Maybe it is not mad, after all. Maybe it is the quiet work of believing in Good. Of believing in a warmth, which you know does not exist in the stars, to exist in the hearts of fellow humans. Maybe it is something like trust.

In this cold, splashing light, a faucet knob turned to the left for over forty-eight hours, it looks almost dignified.

At last, a shipment of ethanol arrived. David hurried to the lab to help his men begin sorting the flesh at their feet. Was that fin . . . did they know it from somewhere? Were those yellow-rimmed eyes, could they place them? This was existential triage. There were species lying on that floor that had not yet been named; if the taxonomists couldn't locate them, there were species that would cease to exist.

David picked up a sloppy brown fish, the width of his palm, with red spots down its back and a bifurcated tail. He stared into one of its marble-black eyes, ransacking the labyrinth of his memory, his many trips all over the globe. *Can I place you?* he wondered. *In a net? Or on a spear? Can I remember where it was you slowly flopped to death, as you became mine?* He paused. He squinted.

And then he had to let go. Flinging the creature away—into the toilet? A trash can? I know not the precise rim of that black hole. It happened once. Then again. A hundred times. A thousand times. A thousand fishes gone. A thousand tiny failures of memory.

Did his frustration cause the innovation?

I don't know. So I am left to imagine that very first stab of the needle. At last, he recognizes a fish—an anchovy-looking thing that looks to me like every fish in every stream. In one hand he holds the miniscule creature, like a jeweler inspecting a diamond. In the other hand, he holds the needle, ready to strike. What was it that David recognized? The faint tiger-striping down its back? The silver rings around its eyes? The tiny pair of pelvic fins, like a translucent butterfly upon its belly? Did he recall those cellophane wings paddling furiously through the water as they tried to evade his net, flapping, flying through mangrove roots, over rippled sand, through that warm, aquamarine water . . . of . . . oh . . . where was it . . . Panama! Yes, that was it, he was sure. He had in his hand the one, the only, the holotype of the Panama goby! *Evermannia panamensis*!

According to the collection records, this was one of the holotypes flung from its jar in the quake, nearly lost to science, but later retrieved. Well, it would never get away from him again.

David would have laced the needle with thread, then plunged the tip through the flesh at the goby's throat and out through the other side. He would have tied a new name tag directly to the flesh itself and, *boom*, the creature would have popped back into existence. *Evermannia panamensis*! That one tiny tendril of Chaos recaptured, thanks to David's unflappable persistence, and brought back into order.

So what was he whispering to himself? As he swept up the shards of his life's work, as he threw away the fishes he could not recognize, as he tucked his little son, Eric, into bed the next night, knowing that lightning and bacteria and tectonic shifts lay in wait—abundantly, eternally—what exactly was he saying to spur himself on, to avoid being crushed under the futility of it all?

I was growing increasingly desperate to know. It had been three years since the curly-haired man left me, and the world continued to whirl with silence. I'd seen him at a wedding; we had hugged, his cinnamon showering down on me. That was it, but I kept hoping. Hoping that someday all could be mended, that our love was strong enough to withstand my betrayal, to withstand years of distance, of no longer knowing one another. It felt good to have faith in something, faith that there are entities that transcended words, actions. Even if that faith was moth-eaten with doubt.

In the intervening years, I had left New York, left my job as a radio reporter. I'd moved to Virginia to seek refuge in a fiction writing program, where I kept imagining my way into the same predicament. I wrote about a narcissistic horseshoe crab that didn't realize why his lover left him. I wrote about a Jill who lost her Jack. I wrote about a woman who strikes up a tremendous friendship with a wall.

When I'd come home to Massachusetts for the holidays, my sisters would each touch my shoulder, in their different ways, and tell me that it was time to move on. My middle sister clutched my shoulder hard, wanting me to buck up, to remember my strength. My oldest sister touched it gently, running her fingers along it as though touching velvet—not wanting, I think, to inflict any more pain. One year, I skipped Christmas altogether. I didn't want to have to face the curly-topped hole of him at our holiday table, didn't want to have to face my sisters' pupils, which were dilating with concern. I stayed in Virginia and tried to hike up to my favorite mountain peak, only to find the road closed because of snow. I sat by the blue metal gate, and looked for a sunset and found only fog.

My apartment in Charlottesville swelled with coffee cups. Each one started out warm and brimming with hope, a hope that I could find the words—for a story, a love letter, a mantra—that would lead me out of the mess. But by the end of each day, the coffee cup would be heavy with cold, grainy soot. So heavy I couldn't lift it. The mugs began accumulating on my windowsills. By the time I finished my thesis, my apartment, a yellow-walled attic, had taken on the sunken smell of soil.

I moved to Chicago. My friend Heather said I could stay in her spare room for a few weeks while I figured out what was next. It was incredibly kind of her. I liked Chicago. The cold of it. The anonymity of it. I could be anyone. I put on Converse sneakers and walked along the gritty sidewalks, which seemed to contain just a dash of carbonation. I bounced. I felt like I could become the person I wanted to be. Not a cheater, not a depressive, not a recipient of cosmic justice. But a person with a happy home at home.

But on nights when Heather was gone, gone with her boyfriend across town, when the city light poured in purple through the window, I'd realize I could not ignore the reality of it all. The emptiness of my life. An emptiness that was only growing wider and colder as I warmed by the light of my hope.

And so. I was desperate. Simply put. I was desperate to come up with some way of continuing forward on what looked like a doomed mission. The precise line in David Starr Jordan's scripture that justified forward momentum on the bleakest of days.

7.

The Indestructible

uckily for me, there was plenty of source material to explore. In addition to David's memoir, there were countless documents—children's stories, philosophical essays, poems, satires, journals, fish-collecting guides, books on humor, on temperance, on diplomacy, syllabi, editorials, and on and on. More than fifty books, all told, and hundreds of other texts.

I started with his children's stories, the place we so often lay bare our moral instruction. There was one called "The Eagle and the Blue-Tailed Skink" (don't think skunk, it's a lizard), in which an eagle swoops down and nips off the tail of a blue-tailed skink. The wounded skink, in vengeance, scurries up to the eagle's nest and devours a bunch of her eggs, thinking, "There is just enough meat in these eggs to make me a new tail." And on they go. The eagle swooping down to bite off a new tail, the lizard scurrying up to gobble more eggs, on and on, neither opponent ever truly vanquished, for there was always, as David writes, "meat enough in the tail to make . . . more eggs, and meat enough in the eggs to make another blue tail." It seems to me like a meditation on the futility of revenge, or perhaps a gory illustration of the most damning laws of physics, the law of conservation of mass: *mass can neither be created nor destroyed.* Most of his stories had this quality. They portrayed a claustrophobic world in which the characters could not escape the cold rules of our universe. In another story, a girl named Barbara is attacked by a coyote that sneaks through her window one night. A gruesome fight scene ensues, ending, finally, when Barbara grabs a doll and stuffs it farther and farther down the coyote's throat until he sneezes and (in cartoonish adherence to Boyle's law, which states that as volume decreases, pressure increases) his head pops off. There was no true magic, even for children. Just survival born of the creative harnessing of these cold, harsh rules.

Finding no secret formula for faith in his children's stories, I moved on to his satires about "sciosophy." What had started as playful, one-off jabs at parapsychologists had blossomed into a full-blown creed that "trying to believe what we know is not true" could be society's downfall. Suffering, sickness, ignorance, and war were just a few of the things David pinned on magical thinking. In a piece called "Science and Sciosophy," published in *Science* in 1924, he hails Giordano Bruno, the sixteenth-century astronomer burned at the stake for believing Earth was not the center of the universe, as a hero. According to legend, before his execution Bruno quipped, "Ignorance is the most delightful science in the world because it is acquired without labor or pains and keeps the mind from melancholy." And David uses the quote to indict his readers, to warn them that if they've ever chosen to shut out hard truths in the name of happiness they are complicit with Bruno's killers.

He was sounding more and more like my father. The way to live was, in every breath, to concede your insignificance, and make your meaning from there. Everywhere I looked, I saw it. Stern warnings against hubris, against magical thinking. In his syllabus for a course on evolution, for example, he sneaks in a whole section on the cosmic impotence of man. "Nature no respecter of persons," he writes. "Tampering impossible. . . . Her laws immutable. . . . He who defies them wields a club of air." I can only imagine the impassioned diatribes that accompanied these notes, his fist held high in the air. His cosmically impotent fist.

You can even find it in his essays on temperance. Why, in the end, was he so opposed to drugs? Because they allow you to feel more powerful than you are! Or, as he puts it, they "forc[e] the nervous system to lie." Alcohol, for example, lets drinkers "feel warm when they are really cold, to feel good without warrant, to feel emancipated from those restraints and reserves which constitute the essence of character building." In other words, a rosy view of yourself was anathema to self-development. A way to keep yourself stagnant, stunted, morally inchoate. A fast track to sad-sackery.

So if this truly was his worldview, if he was so wary of over-confidence, how on earth did he manufacture his persistence? How did he get himself up and out the door on the worst of days, when everything seemed lost, crumbled, hopeless?

At last I got my hands on what looked like the most promising lead. A small black book called *The Philosophy of Despair*. In it, David confesses that the trouble with the scientific worldview was that when you pointed it at the meaning of life, it showed you one thing. Futility: "The fires we kindle die away in coals; castles we build vanish before our eyes. The river sinks in the sands of the desert. . . . Whichever way we turn we may describe the course of life in metaphors of discouragement." So what were you supposed to do?

Puritan that he is, David recommends the un-idling of hands. The "soul-ache . . . vanishes," he writes, "with active out-of-door life and the consequent flow of good health." He claims that salvation lies in the electricity of our bodies. "Happiness comes from doing, helping, working, loving, fighting, conquering," he writes in a syllabus from around the same time, "from the exercise of functions; from self-activity." Don't overthink it, I think, is his point. Enjoy the journey. Savor the small things. The "luscious" taste of a peach, the "lavish" colors of tropical fish, the rush from exercise that allows one to experience "the stern joy which warriors feel." Toward the end of the book, he quotes Thoreau—"There is no hope for you unless this bit of sod under your feet is the sweetest to you in this world—in any world"—and then he sends his readers off with a rousing chant of carpe diem. "Nowhere is the sky so blue, the grass so green, the sunshine so bright, the shade so welcome, as right here, now, today."

And what if you're having a bad day? Well, David has very little sympathy for people having bad days. The ultimate conclusion of *The Philosophy of Despair* is that despair is a choice. While he thinks it's a natural phase of adolescence, he mocks those who can't shake it. He calls them lazy, whiny posers who are putting on the "fad of the drooping spirit" to imitate the "'sad kings'" of literature. He accuses them of having "sulphurous" [*sic*] breath. The whiff of death. He says that the problem with spending one's time pondering the futility of it all is that you divert that precious electricity gifted to you by evolution—those sacred ions that could make you feel so many wonderful sensations and think so many wonderful ideas— and you flush it all down the drain of existential inquiry, causing you to literally "die while the body is still alive."

I felt a familiar shame washing over me. It was the same feeling I'd get when I'd watch my dad belly-flop into a frigid lake and emerge whooping with a frothy smile. Why was I so unable to live like him? What was I doing wrong? Desperate for an answer, I kept reading, ransacking David's diatribes on hygiene, on humor, on diplomacy, on pacifism, his poems, his lecture notes, his polemics against alcohol and lipstick and war. And finally, one afternoon, I found it.

An antidote to terror. A recipe for hope. It was buried at the bottom of a syllabus for a course he taught called Philosophy of Evolution. It turned out that he devoted a whole course day to my very conundrum, the problem with accepting the scientific worldview: "Do these views of life lead to Pessimism?" Toward the end of his lecture, he offers his students a kind of magic spell. A way of diffusing the chill of Chaos. In Courier type, just thirty-one letters long: *There is grandeur in this view of life.*

I was horrified. There it was. My dad's very same trick. The words that hang in a frame over his desk, to this very day. Darwin's call to arms. As different as David had seemed from my dad—as defiant, and hopeful, and full of faith—he had nothing new to offer me after all. Just a reminder of what I'd always been told. There *is* grandeur, and if you can't see it, shame on you.

I decided to do the thing that best helped me hope. Drink. Red wine or beer or whiskey. I didn't care. I was still in Chicago. It had been two months. Now it was December. I was freelancing, writing for a science blog and filing as many radio stories as I could. I did one about violence in crickets. One about violence in humans. One about violence in ticks. Heather and I filled the evenings by cooking, watching movies, sometimes going to talks. I'd make sure each activity came with an alcoholic beverage, and another, and another. It felt great to feel *warmth without warrant.* I could rediscover my laughter, the springs that made my smile go. When I'd awake the next morning, the world would feel extra bleak, yes, my face extra puffy and unlovable, yes, but I'd just wait till evening, when I could try to make it all go sparkly again.

One night, I met a friend, Stanzi, at a bar in Rogers Park. We ordered stouts and started talking about our work. She was working on a project to make poetry work on the radio. We started talking about the ideas-words divide. How hard it can be to watch your words fall flat, *kersplat,* before another person. How lonely it can feel inside a head with ideas you can't figure out how to spit out. And the dangerous power of the few who seemed to understand you. I told her about my obsession with David Starr Jordan, the earthquake, the sewing needle. "So it's sort of about *why*," I said. "What drives a person to keep going?"

All she said was "Huh" in the moment, and I felt a little deflated, but a longer reply came the next afternoon, via email:

> and your story—the man who builds something so precious, so ornate . . . only to see it all crumble . . . where does he re-locate his will to go on? Kafka calls it the Indestructible—the thing at the bottom of each individual that keeps going whether they feel like going or not. The Indestructible is a place that has nothing to do with optimism—instead, it's something far deeper and far less self-conscious than optimism—the Indestructible is the thing we mask with all sorts of other symbols, hopes, and ambitions—that don't force you to acknowledge what is underneath. Well . . . if you do (or are forced to) remove all those excesses, you get the Indestructible, and once you acknowledge it, Kafka goes deeper—he doesn't let you think the Indestructible is optimistic or positive—instead it is the thing that could actually rip us apart and destroy us . . .
>
> And so it goes . . .

I loved it. *The Indestructible.* It was a glorious concept because it gave me permission to not have to answer the question of if I was mad to keep charging toward unrealistic goals. It promised simply that if I disobeyed it, it would tear me apart. But I didn't think it quite fit David Starr Jordan. The Indestructible seemed like an affliction for Fools. Romantics. Sad-King-Loving Posers so fueled by an internal passion it could fog up their view of the world. But

David Starr Jordan? No way. His entire lifework was committed to wiping *away* the steam that such passion can leave upon the lenses of the eyes.

But I wanted to make sure. So I went back to his memoir. Armed with this new word, "Indestructible"—supposedly animating ideas formerly inert to me—I searched for evidence of it, hiding in David's descriptions. I reread the sections about Rufus's death, Susan's death, Barbara's death, the lightning strike, the earthquake, and then I saw it.

Buried in a lengthy excerpt in microscopic font. It was a quotation of his own work—a personal essay he had written just a few days after the earthquake, while he was still raw, trying to process the extent of the damage to San Francisco.

> Never since man began to plan and to create has there been such a destruction of the results of human effort. Never has a great calamity been met with so little repining. Never before has the common man shown himself so hopeful, so courageous, so sure of himself and his future. For it is man, after all, that survives and it is the will of man that shapes the fates.
>
> It is the lesson of earthquake and fire that man cannot be shaken and cannot be burned. The houses he builds are houses of cards, but he stands outside of them and can build again. It is a wonderful thing to build a great city. More wonderful still is it to be a city, for a city is composed of men, and forever man must rise above his own creations. That which is in man is greater than all that he can do.

What a wonderful, rousing call to arms. What a glorious pat on the back, and squeeze of the shoulders. With only one tiny problem.

If you examine his words closely, you will discover it. The tiny grain of sand that forms the pearl is a lie.

It is the will of man that shapes the fates.

It was the kind of lie he promised he would never tell himself. It was the kind of lie he had warned would lead to evil. It was the kind of lie he had spent his career crusading against—*Nature no respecter of persons!*—the kind of lie he said was worth fighting to the death. Even he needed to believe it was true, so as not to be consumed by despair.

8.

On Delusion

o there it was. As David swept up the glass in his lab, as he began to try to piece his life back together, the thing he was whispering to himself was a lie.

It is the will of man that shapes the fates.

It was shocking to see, a surprise based on everything he stood for. But considering the fact that David ultimately ended up being able to salvage so much of his collection, considering that thousands of specimens remain today over a century later, considering that by so many measures David Starr Jordan's life turned out to be one of unusual success—the wives, the presidencies, the awards, the Garden of Eden complete with dog-riding monkeys and Latin-speaking parrots and taxonomy-loving children—I was beginning to wonder if self-delusion *was* such a bad thing. Maybe he and my father didn't need to be so moralistic about it, calling it a sin to avoid at all costs.

I decided to put my morality on the shelf for a moment and see what the professionals had to say about the matter: Was self-delusion as dangerous as David and my father warned?

For a long time, society's moral authorities would have said yes. The Bible, I've heard, looks down on self-delusion, calling hubris a cardinal sin and promising that if you forgo it, you'll get the best goodie of all: *The meek shall inherit the Earth.* The ancient Greeks, too, were famously opposed to hubris—Icarus tumbling down from the sky, waxed and feathered by the sun. By the Enlightenment, Voltaire was decrying optimism as a most insidious evil for how it made you blind to suffering. By the twentieth century, the medical experts concurred. Self-delusion was seen as a mental defect by influential psychologists like Freud, Maslow, and Erikson, a problem in vision to be corrected with therapy. An accurate view, on the other hand, was seen as a "hallmark of mental health."

But as the twentieth century roared on, clinical psychologists began noticing odd things. Their healthier patients, the ones leading easier lives, bouncing back more quickly after setbacks, getting jobs, friends, lovers, all the gold rings on the carousel of life, seemed to carry the rosy mark of self-delusion. So starting in the 1970s, a wave of researchers began running experiments to see if it was true. And time and time again they found that, indeed, mentally healthy people rated themselves as more attractive than they were, more helpful, more intelligent, more in control of chance events (like rolling dice or picking winning lottery numbers) than they possibly could be. When they looked into their past, they remembered their successes with more ease than their failures. When they looked into their future, they voted themselves as more likely to succeed than their friends and classmates.

Those people, on the other hand, with that oh-so-hailed virtue of accurate perception? *Ding ding ding*, you guessed it: clinically depressed. They struggled in their lives, found it harder to recoup after setbacks, often had more trouble in work and relationships.

So a few modifications were made in the *Diagnostic and Statistical Manual of Mental Disorders*. A few traits slid from the proverbial unhealthy column to the healthy one. The term "delusions" was neutered to "positive illusions." And by the late 1980s, largely because of a seminal paper by psychologists Shelley Taylor and Jonathon Brown that reviewed over two hundred studies that had shown a range of benefits of living with a positively warped worldview, it became widely accepted that a dash of self-deception . . . was good for the bones.

All this, maybe you've heard. What you might not know is that this change in belief about how a healthy person should be oriented to reality changed what goes on in the therapist's office. Many therapists started practicing techniques like "story editing" or "reframing" to gently coax a patient into tinting her perception of herself into a more rosy one. The self-deception had to be moderate, that was key. Multiple studies found that extreme denial and delusion were maladaptive. But gentle lies, white lies, little rosy rosebuds of lies? Those could be hugely beneficial. The idea was that if you could take a person who was struggling, and help guide her story of herself into a slightly more positive one—one in which she was a bit stronger than she was, kinder than she was, where her breakup was not as much her fault as maybe it was—then you could see *profound* effects in her life.

Tim Wilson, a psychologist at the University of Virginia, was so bowled over by how small adjustments in narrative could change a life that he wrote a whole book, called *Redirect*, compiling some of the most dramatic effects. College students who received "story-editing interventions" got better grades, dropped out of school less, even had better health years later. Workers who underwent story-editing interventions started showing up to work more. Traumatized people taught to tweak their story of what had happened made their way more quickly to a sense of peace.

"Does it matter that you're lying to yourself?" I asked Wilson.

"What's the harm?" he replied. "If it conquers a fear and doesn't lead to maladaptive behaviors in the future, I see no problem with it."

"A little lie can go a long way?"

"Sure."

As I read through this seemingly bottomless Mary Poppins bag of goodies that positive illusions could apparently bring—deeper sense of well-being, more success at work and in relationships, even better physical health—it dawned on me that perhaps my dad had steered me astray with his insistence on nose-to-the-ants humility. Perhaps the greatest gift ever bestowed on us by evolution is the ability to believe we are more powerful than we are. It's a hard lot being a human, these psychologists explain. You walk around with the knowledge that the world is fundamentally uncaring, that no matter how hard you work there is no promise of success, that you are competing against billions, that you are vulnerable to the elements, and that everything you ever love will eventually be destroyed. A little lie can take the edge off, can help you keep charging forward into the gauntlet of life, where you sometimes, accidentally, prevail.

As the 1980s whirled on, snap bracelets, neon shirts, and parenting books containing tactics for inflating a child's self-esteem were pressed, printed, and purchased. What had formally been viewed with suspicion was now being prescribed in psychologists' offices, scooped heartily into teaching manuals, and folded into elementary school curricula.

The 1990s brought Pogs, Magic cards, and a statement in a National Institute of Mental Health report that "considerable evidence suggests positive psychological benefits for people who believe their future will be rosier than they have any right to expect. Such optimism keeps people in a positive mood, motivates them to work toward future goals, fosters creative, productive work, and gives them a sense of being in control of their destiny."

By the early 2000s, a high school math teacher named Angela Duckworth had decided to get her doctorate in psychology. For years, she had wondered why some of her students seemed to struggle more than others. She wanted to figure out what it was that the achievers had. A few years later, she unearthed a trait she named "grit" that seemed to be the magic ingredient. Grit. A catchier word for persistence. Grit. The robotic plunging at "extremely long-term objectives" without "positive feedback." Grit. The ability to bang one's head repeatedly against a wall. She'd seen it in West Point cadets and CEOs and people at the top of their game in every profession. Musicians. Athletes. Chefs. Forget talent, creativity, kindness, IQ. Pure grit seemed to be the thing that would get you ahead.

And what cognitive glitch helps you achieve grit? Positive illusions. Other studies showed that if you had positive illusions, you were less likely to experience discouragement after setbacks. And while grit is a cocktail of many traits, one of its most important ones is just that: an ability to keep going after setbacks, to keep going in the face of no evidence that what you are striving for will ever work, or, as Duckworth puts it, "maintaining effort and interest over years despite failure, adversity, and plateaus in progress."

Perhaps the best part of grit, its most hopeful attribute, the one that squared most nicely with the American dream, was that it did not appear to be biologically based. Grit, this magical quality that could turn dreams into reality, could be taught! Type "grit" into Amazon today, and you will find a long list of how-to books.

Grit: How to Keep Going When You Want to Give Up

Grit: The New Science of What It Takes to Persevere, Flourish, Succeed

Grit to Great: How Perseverance, Passion, and Pluck Take You from Ordinary to Extraordinary

A little bottle pops up, too. A little black pill bottle with neon-green lettering that says: "True GRIT Test Booster." Inside are 120 tablets of "science-based, research-backed, fully disclosed and results-oriented supplements" that will improve your physical performance from "the gym . . . to the streets."

I thought of the very first photo I ever saw of David Starr Jordan. The one of him with his wild white hair and hardened gaze. I thought of the "shield of optimism" he was so proud to possess, of the colleague who said that no matter how bad the day David could always be found "humming a tune adown the arcade." In many ways, he is the poster child for grit. Nearly quoting Duckworth's definition of the trait, David described himself this way: "I became accustomed to work persistently toward desired ends and then take the upshot calmly. Moreover, I never worry over a mischance, once it is past." Indeed, throughout his life, you can watch him fending off misfortune in real time. He's a sort of Rumpelstiltskin of the Dis. Able to take any rejection, insult, or failure and magically transform it into a compliment. At one point in his memoir, he effortlessly transmutes a string of failures into a bouquet of compliments. In college, he lost the Botany Prize because, as he explains, his thinking was too expansive for standardized tests; he lost the Entomology Prize because he was too generous (he "stood back" to let a poorer student win the money); and the French History Prize he lost because he was too ethical (forfeiting his chance to try when he decided its rules were "unfair"). Historian Luther Spoehr, who wrote his dissertation on David Starr Jordan, noticed the same phenomenon, how he had a knack for slyly editing out or omitting information that would hurt his self-image.

It's remarkable to watch how deftly David fends off potential character attacks. Breathtaking, almost. Like watching an acrobat soar through the air, pulling flips and turns that seem impossible. There he goes, encountering the ugly fact of his beloved Charley's sexual indiscretions. Can he possibly do it? Stay airborne? Not let the information puncture his lofty view of himself and his associates? Out of nowhere, it seems, he grabs a trapeze, a handhold, a way of keeping himself afloat. He will accuse the accuser of "sexual perversity!" And like that—*poof*—the accusation disappears! When

Jane Stanford accuses him of nepotism, he admits to never open-ing that "trunk . . . full of applications for positions in the faculty," but says he did so to *help* the university. Since his friends were the greatest scientists in all the land, what use would it be to consider strangers? *Voilà!* The criticism becomes proof of his virtue.

As you watch David go, you begin to wonder if he ever feels the stings of criticism. Or has he become so adept at wielding his trusty shield that they never even touch his heart?

Whatever the case, it works for him. He loses a wife, and wins another quickly. He loses a fish collection, and rebuilds a bigger one. He is promoted to higher and higher offices. The awards and med-als start clattering in, for teaching, for ichthyology, for contributions to higher ed. An odd alchemy of delusion right before your eyes. Little lies transmuting into bronze, silver, gold. Forget millennia of warnings to stay humble; maybe this is just how it works in a god-less system. Maybe David Starr Jordan is proof that a steady dose of hubris is the best way of overcoming doomed odds.

"Every age gets the lunatics it deserves," British historian Roy Por-ter once wrote.

So what will become of us?

This nation programming its kids to ignore reality when conve-nient. To whisper anything they need to keep themselves going. Is there any downside to living life behind rose-colored lenses?

It turns out there is a small army of researchers, scattered across the country, investigating just that. Their methodologies are fun to imagine. They follow cocky people around their offices and school-yards, clipboards in hand, tallying up their every social foible. And their results complicate the idea that positive illusions bring forth unmitigated good. Delroy Paulhus found that while college stu-

dents are initially drawn to those students with inflated self-esteem, over time the group grows weary of them, rating them more negatively. Tomas Chamorro-Premuzic found that overconfidence has serious costs in the workplace. One of the most widely cited studies claiming that positive illusions correlate with better physical health turned out to contain errors that rendered the results not significant. Michael Dufner, who did a meta-analysis of hundreds of studies on "self-enhancement," found that over time, an overconfident person's boasting can end up alienating others; while the overconfident person might not ever realize it, they may be losing out on benefits that come from being well-regarded in a community. There may be fewer rakes lent, fewer invitations to potlucks, fewer positive recommendations for jobs.

But it's not just the social toll. Inside the thick-walled bubble of self-delusion, the pain can slowly accumulate. Wilberta Donovan found that new mothers with a high illusion of control experienced more feelings of helplessness when their babies wouldn't stop crying than do their depressive counterparts. Richard Robins and Jennifer Beer looked at college students over four years and found that, while students with high positive illusions were happier in the short term (because they thought they did better on tasks than they actually did), over time their ratings of well-being took a nosedive. You're setting yourself up for disappointment, was how Robins and Beer explained it: "short-term benefits but long-term costs." In other words, the lie catches up. The power of the rosy lens seems to have a limit. And when it runs out, the fact of your impotence will really sting.

I think of these psychologists as the quiet, ragtag troop of Cheerleaders for Low Self-Worth.

Their pom-poms are droopy.

They whisper when they cheer.

Be HUMBLE! Be BLUE!

Who's the best??

NOT YOU!

And their head cheerleader, with his head hung, is probably Roy Baumeister. He's a psychologist who found his way into this stuff when he began looking into the psychological causes of aggression. While the traditional wisdom had been, as Baumeister explains, "that low self-esteem underlies aggression," he wanted to make sure. So he grabbed a bunch of college students with varying levels of self-esteem, insulted them, and waited to see who would lash out. Their violence, by the way, he measured by seeing how loudly they blasted an obnoxious sound at people. To noise-blast or not to noise-blast, 'tis the question. And he saw something shocking. Something that, because it came on the heels of such a widespread effort to inflate children's self-esteem, troubled him greatly.

That it was people with a grandiose view of themselves who strike out. In other words, Baumeister and his colleague Brad J. Bushman discovered what depressed people had known all along. If you tell a person with low self-esteem "You suck," they say "You're right," and roll back under the covers. It's the esteem-bloated person, who has enough belief in himself to classify such an insult as untrue, who bothers striking back.

"Aggressors often think very highly of themselves," Baumeister and Bushman write, "as evidenced by nationalistic imperialism, 'master race' ideologies, aristocratic dueling, playground bullies, and street gang rhetoric." Odd, too, how many people who might score high on tests for positive illusions share a peculiar quirk with David Starr Jordan, a belief that they can control Chaos with their very own hands. Fidel Castro once proposed building a shield around Cuba to protect it from hurricanes. Moscow mayor Yury Luzhkov wanted to stop snowfall by spraying a chemical mist of cement upon the clouds. And speaking of cement barriers, there was once a man of some power in this country who wanted to build a "physically imposing" wall made of concrete or steel to protect against a force as inevitable, and enriching, as wind.

Baumeister and Bushman are quick to point out that not all high self-esteem is bad. They often find themselves needing to explain, palms in the air, that high self-esteem can be great! High self-esteem, they say, can make you freakishly peaceful (or "exceptionally nonaggressive," as they put it), because you're so comfortable with yourself that criticism does not threaten your self-worth. They believe it's the very small subset of people with *easily threatened* high self-esteem that are the dangerous ones.

"In plainer terms," Baumeister and Bushman write, "it is not so much the people who regard themselves as superior beings who are the most dangerous but, rather, those who have a strong desire to regard themselves as superior beings. . . . People who are preoccupied with validating a grandiose self-image apparently find criticism highly upsetting and lash out against the source of it."

I thought back to the eerie fish I had seen at Stanford, the one fish in the sea David Starr Jordan had named after himself. The spiny Möbius-strip of a dragon, with two opposing sides curled seamlessly into one. Jordan of the No Corners. Was there a message hidden in his choice? A nod to a dark side underlying his charm?

"One of Jordan's most double-edged talents," writes Luther Spoehr, "was his ability to persuade himself that he was doing the right thing and then pursue his goal with seemingly boundless energy. . . . He prided himself on his tolerance and liberality . . . but . . . Jordan was not reluctant to use a cannon to swat a fly."

9.

The Bitterest Thing in the World

Let's return to 1905. A year before the earthquake. When David's fish collection was still standing tall but his presidency was looking like it could topple. Jane Stanford's spy had written up the damning report accusing David of "whitewashing" a sex scandal and running the university like the leader of a "gang." The report had been circulated to the board of trustees, and rumors were flying that Jane was about to fire him.

It was odd timing, then, that just a couple of weeks into the year, Jane Stanford was poisoned. According to reports, on January 14, 1905, she was at home in her San Francisco town house, getting ready for bed, when she took a big swig of water poured from her usual source, the tank of Poland Spring water in her kitchen. She tasted something so alarming and astringent that she immediately stuck her fingers down her throat to force vomiting. She summoned her assistants, Bertha and Elizabeth, to help. After calming her, they both tasted the water and, noting a "queer" and "bitter" taste, took the tank to a nearby chemist, who analyzed it and found it contained lethal amounts of strychnine.

Jane survived but was understandably shaken. A detective turned up no leads; the investigation had focused solely on her household staff—the maid, the cook, the secretary, the ex-butler—and ended up clearing everybody. A novelist, paid to speculate on the intentions of the poisoner for the *San Francisco Examiner*, speculated it must have been done by a subordinate of Jane's who had been "brooding over the intellectual and other defects of the employer" for so long that the "contempt galled by the chain of servitude" had grown into "the most murderous hatred of all." Knowing there was someone out there who wanted her dead, but not knowing *who*, Jane set sail for Hawaii, hoping that a few weeks in the tropics would calm her nerves. She brought her longtime secretary, Bertha, and a new maid, May, and they all settled into two rooms at the Moana Hotel, a lavish new resort with Ionic columns, ornate balconies, and an electric-powered elevator, right on the shores of Waikiki.

According to weather data, the last day of Jane's life was a stunner. Sunny, highs in the sixties. Jane and her entourage, who had been on the island for about a week, decided to take a carriage up to the Pali overlook for a scenic picnic. They brought with them a picnic basket prepared by the hotel's kitchen staff containing freshly baked gingerbread, hard-boiled eggs, meat-and-cheese sandwiches, chocolates, and coffee. For a few hours, they sat in the shade, enjoying the ocean view, picking at their snacks, and reading aloud to one another from a sci-fi novel.

In the late afternoon, they returned to the hotel, rested for a bit, and had a light dinner of soup. Then, as Jane was readying herself for bed, she asked Bertha to leave out her medications—baking soda and herbal cascara capsules to help with digestion. Bertha left out a spoonful of baking soda and one cascara capsule, and around 9:00 p.m. she and May retired to their room across the hall.

Frogs chirping. Waves lapping. Slumber.

At approximately 11:15, Jane's assistants were awakened by cries coming from across the hall. "Bertha! May!" Jane called. "I am so sick!" They hurried to Jane's room, opened the door, and found Jane keeled over. She was having trouble opening her mouth, her jaw muscles beginning to clamp down against her will. Through widened eyes and barricaded teeth, Jane bleated, "I have no control of my body. I think I have been poisoned again." The baking soda spoon gleamed empty on her bedside table. By that point, the man staying next door, having heard the commotion, had rushed over to help. He ran for a doctor. A few minutes later, a sleepy, doe-eyed Dr. Francis Humphris arrived, medicine bag in hand. He sat with Jane, gently palpating her jaw, trying to coax her muscles into relaxing, and finally yanking out her dentures so he could give her some mustard water to induce vomiting. But it was no use. Jane looked at Dr. Humphris with eyes wide as her body began to contort in stranger and stranger ways. Her toes pigeoned inward, her fists clenched into rocks, and her legs splayed open into an unseemly spread-eagle. Helpless, horrified, she stared at something, somewhere just beyond or within her, and pleaded through toothless gums, "Oh God, forgive me my sins." She was dead, only fifteen minutes after it had all begun, by 11:30.

Two more doctors arrived a few minutes later. One with a stomach pump dangling uselessly from his hand. All three doctors tasted the baking soda remaining in the bottle and noted a foreign, bitter taste. The sheriff arrived and wrapped the spoon and glass in paper and sent them to the toxicologist's office, and sent Jane's body to the morgue. Seven physicians were called in to conduct the autopsy because of the high-profile nature of the case; they scanned Jane's skin, searching for evidence of cuts or abrasions, but finding none, they ruled out tetanus, which could have explained the convulsions and lockjaw. The chief pathologist on the case, Clifford Brown Wood, was so struck by the rigidity of Jane's fists that he just kept uncoiling her fingers and watching them recoil. Uncoil. Recoil. Uncoil. Recoil. The toxicologists got to work examining the contents of the bottle of baking soda and the contents of Jane's intestines. They found traces of strychnine in both.

A jury of six citizens was convened, shown the body, and then made to sit through three days of testimony. They heard from the toxicologist, who had seen the bright red indicative of strychnine appear on the chemical test he performed on her organs. They heard from the chemist, who had watched as hard white octahedral crystals of strychnine precipitated out of a solution made from her bottle of baking soda. From the seasoned physician who said the immediate rigidity of Jane's muscles was far more extreme than rigor mortis and "a condition that I don't recall having seen before [in twenty years of practicing medicine] on any body." They heard from three eyewitnesses: Bertha, May, and Dr. Humphris, who each said they watched Jane convulse to death in a matter of minutes.

It took the jury two minutes to settle on a verdict. Jane Stanford, they decided, had died from "strychnine having been introduced into a bottle of bicarbonate of soda with felonious intent by some person or persons to this jury unknown."

The newspapers scooped the jury and printed the finding ahead of the verdict. MRS. STANFORD DIES, POISONED, blared the front page of the *San Francisco Evening Bulletin* on March 1, 1905.

David Starr Jordan, however, from over a thousand miles away on California's coast, did not agree. Upon learning that the death would likely be ruled a poisoning, he set sail for Hawaii. He told the *New York Times* his visit had "nothing whatever to do with the investigation which the police of San Francisco and Honolulu are conducting," that he was there only to escort Jane's body home. But records show he hired a new doctor and paid him the hefty sum of $350—about $10,000 today—to reexamine the case. The man David selected had only been practicing medicine for a couple of years. His name was Ernest Waterhouse, and though he never examined the body or any of the evidence, after a skim of a book on poisoning, conversations with a couple of the witnesses, and a series of meetings with David, in his hands the explanation of Jane's death took an acrobatic turn. In a typed memo to David (which David had instructed he prepare for him), Dr. Waterhouse declared that he was "decidedly not" convinced that Jane Stanford had been poisoned. What concerned him was the *amount* of strychnine found in her belly and bottle. He wasn't sure it was enough to have killed her.

So how to explain the violent convulsions, the lockjaw, the whole . . . rapid death . . . thing?

Pause.

Gingerbread!

After Jane's secretary, Bertha, was interviewed a second time, that picnic on the Pali transformed into a grotesque feast of rancid gingerbread. Now Bertha said that the gingerbread had not been freshly cooked, as she had originally testified to the police (and the hotel continued to claim), but undercooked. Jane had not stopped eating the bread upon discovering its supposedly wet center but instead kept going, inhaling gob after gob of the sloppy, eggy dough. And apparently that still wasn't enough. According to this new interview with Bertha, Jane then sucked down *eight* sandwiches, filled with thick slabs of beef tongue and Swiss cheese, multiple cups of cold coffee, and over a dozen French candies. How does a picnic turn into a feeding frenzy in just one interview? Is it coercion, suggestion, confession? I don't know. All I know is that after a couple of days on the island, David Starr Jordan had become "morally certain" that Jane Stanford had not been maliciously poisoned but had instead died from overconsumption. He informed the *New York Times* that he was "wholly convinced" her death was due to heart failure triggered by a combination of overexertion (from reclining on a picnic blanket?) and consuming "a surfeit of unsuitable food."

✳   ✳   ✳

"You *could* die from eating too much gingerbread," Seema Yasmin, a doctor and former disease detective for the CDC, told me when I called her to ask about the details of Jane's case. "But eleven hours later?"

She was very stuck on the time delay. She said *anything* can become toxic at the right dose ("I mean, you can die from drinking too much water!"), but she didn't think two or three servings of even raw gingerbread would do the trick. As for the combination of overeating and overexertion causing some sort of heart failure, again, she said it was possible, but it would have likely happened right there at the picnic. "People have a heart attack when they are *on* the phone with the electricity company having a big fight. And they're very stressed out and they have angina, and that emotional stress causes the heart vessels to spasm, and then they have a heart attack. But *eleven hours* earlier, and then it happens?"

She paused.

"That doesn't sound so feasible."

She asked if tetanus had been considered, and I told her they had ruled it out after finding no cuts on Jane's skin.

When I finally told her that small amounts of strychnine had been found in Jane's intestines and medicine bottle, she said, "Oh."

Then: "Wow, it seems a lot like a strychnine poisoning." She told me that strychnine is known as "the poison of Hollywood films. Because it's that poison that does what you see in the movies: where somebody's eyes are rolling back in their heads and they can't control their body, and they're having seizures—these, like, *very dramatic* contortions where their body's twisting this way and that. That's what this poison does."

She told me that even miniscule amounts can kill within five minutes of exposure.

"Hmmm . . . ," I said.

I began running her through the physicians' notes made about Jane's heart. There were terms I didn't understand and I wanted to make sure I wasn't missing something that would point to heart failure. I told her about the presence of cyanic blood found in the chambers, the insignificant amount of athermanous plaques of the mitral and semilunar valves, but nothing jumped out at her. "Look," she said once I reached the end of the list, "you could argue that at the end of the day, we're all going to die of our hearts not beating anymore, because that's how we define death. Unless it's brain death. But, no, it doesn't sound like angina or myocarditis. Or even a heart attack. I'm sure she had a heart attack, you know, during that whole process, her heart muscle would have been impacted, too. But it's just . . . the overall picture. It sounds a lot like strychnine poisoning."

David Starr Jordan, however, without access to CDC detectives from the future, much preferred the explanation he had helped pay for—death by natural causes. Four days after landing on the island, he told the *New York Times* that as "a doctor of medicine" (a degree he himself had once called "scarcely earned") he was "more sure than ever that she was not poisoned."

Her death? Due to gingerbread.

The presence of strychnine in her body and medicine bottle? He explained it away as "medicinal."

There was just one more detail left, then, to explain away. Perhaps the most damning piece of evidence of all. An eyewitness account reported from inside the very body beginning to malfunction. As the electricity of Jane's body began to betray her—commanding her legs spread open, her jaw slam shut—she managed to grab control of her tongue to steer out a crucial message: "I think I have been poisoned again."

To that, David and Dr. Waterhouse came up with a most logical explanation: "hysteria." Of course. Jane was faking being poisoned! Faking the convulsions! Faking the ... death? How marvelous it is to watch the acrobat as he flips through the air, pulling turns and accomplishing the seemingly impossible, to gaslight even someone's experience of death.

On his final morning on the island, David awoke in his hotel room, pulled out a stack of hotel stationery, and began composing a public statement that he hoped would permanently debunk the theory of murder. He scribbled down a few words, then crossed a bunch of them out. He decided to remove any mention of the previous poisoning attempt—better if that wasn't on people's minds. He declared his medical certainty that Jane had died of natural causes, a combination of gluttony and overexertion. He concluded by laying thick praise on the Hawaii doctors whose medical opinions he was calling into question, thanking them for being "generous-hearted," "helpful and sympathetic." He then signed the statement, sealed it, and gave it to a lawyer friend, instructing him to wait until *after* he set sail for home so he wouldn't risk any awkward confrontations with the doctors.

After that, David had just one thing left to do. He threw on a nice suit, washed his hands of ink, strolled over to the Central Union Church in Honolulu, and slipped his freshly scrubbed palm around the cold handle of Jane Stanford's coffin. He took a deep breath and braced his quads for the honor of serving as one of her pallbearers.

When David's statement hit the newspapers, the Hawaii doctors were horrified. They banded together and immediately released a counterstatement, which read:

She did not die of angina pectoris because neither the symptoms of the attack nor the condition of the heart confirms that diagnosis. It is imbecile to think that a woman of Mrs. Stanford's age and known mental characteristics might have died of an hysterical seizure in half an hour. . . . No Board of Health in existence could allow a certificate based on such a cause of death to go unchallenged.

"Imbecile!?" David immediately struck back, calling the key medical witness, Dr. Humphris, "a man without professional or personal standing." When the Hawaii doctors rushed to Humphris's defense, David accused them all of colluding in a conspiracy—fabricating the diagnosis of murder as a way of getting money to perform the autopsy and coroner's inquest. A ludicrous accusation, if you think about the number of people who would have had to have been in on it (not just the various doctors but the random hotel guest who rushed to Jane's room, Jane's secretary, her maid, the sheriff, the undertaker, the coroner). No matter.

Because of David's prestige, his power, a nation's disregard for its islands, something, the Hawaii doctors' account of what happened never really took hold on the mainland.

You won't find much about the possibility of murder if you look on Stanford's web page. Jane Stanford's death is listed as "never conclusively determined." And way down in a long profile of David Starr Jordan called "Meet President Jordan," you'll find one sentence about his potential involvement in Jane Stanford's death: "When she died under mysterious circumstances in February 1905, Jordan rushed to Hawaii to claim the body—and, some believe, to quash reports that she had been poisoned." Although even these allusions are recent additions. For nearly a century, it was widely accepted that Jane had died of natural causes; any rumors of more nefarious explanations had been so effectively discounted they had pretty much disappeared.

I learned about it all from a slim, gray, meticulously researched book called *The Mysterious Death of Jane Stanford*, published in 2003 by Robert W. P. Cutler, MD. Toward the end of his life, Robert Cutler, a Stanford neurologist, had stumbled across an old newspaper article about an investigation into the poisoning of Jane Stanford while researching another project. Robert was shocked. He was a history buff and a proud Stanford man. Why had he never heard that the founding mother had potentially been poisoned? So he began digging. He could see from online databases that there were autopsy reports, court transcripts, eyewitness testimonies, just sitting out there in Hawaii ready to be examined.

However, by that point in his life, Robert could not safely leave his mountaintop home in Livermore, California. He had advanced emphysema and had to stay indoors, away from dust, tethered to an oxygen tank. So with the help of his wife, Maggie, and a flock of archivists from Honolulu to San Francisco to Washington, DC, he had documents scanned and mailed or (when it was Maggie) hand-delivered to the safety of his home office, where he set to the work of reading through them and writing up his findings.

There's not a spare word in the book he put together. No dramatic speculation on people's motives or emotional states. Just the evidence, laid out as clearly as possible, with long quotations from the primary sources themselves. You feel that you are hearing the voices of the past speaking directly to you. The coroner's report, the eyewitness testimonies, the court transcripts, you hear them all. The book's slimness is his gift to the future, his attempt to sift truth from bullshit. He was able to get everything off to the presses and see the first edition come out into the world, and then he died.

In his book, Robert Cutler, a medical doctor for more than three decades, is clear: given Jane's symptoms and the discovery of strychnine in both her belly and medicine bottle, he believes she was poisoned. And after tracing David Starr Jordan's actions in the wake of her death, he believes it's hard not to conclude that David was trying to cover up the poisoning. Why? Perhaps to protect the university from scandal. Perhaps for other reasons. Robert Cutler won't wager a guess.

Other scholars go further. Bliss Carnochan, a Stanford English professor who studied the letters between Jane and her spy, thought the timing of the murder was fishy. He wrote that David, as a means of protecting his presidency, "had the motive." Richard White, a Stanford historian, began teaching a class called Who Killed Jane Stanford? to try to uncover more clues. Each semester, he unleashes a dozen students or so on the archives to find new information. White's current guess is that Bertha did it (for the will money), but he remarks that the timing of Jane's death was remarkably "lucky" for David. He feels increasingly confident that, no matter who did it, David covered up the poisoning. His students keep uncovering more of David's shady behavior in the wake of Jane's death: the letter from David's acquaintance assuring him that it *is* possible to die from eating too much food, the letter from an unknown person telling David he will be "judged in the afterlife" for covering up a crime, the letter from Jane's spy telling David his "silence can't be bought." There's also the oddness of David's continuing to insist that Jane had died of natural causes, decades after anybody was suggesting otherwise. It crops up in weird places—speeches, newspaper articles, letters—as David ages. White wonders why David would go to such lengths to keep asserting this version of events. It seems to White that something about Jane's death was still preying on David, all the way to the end.

It was a long drive up to Robert Cutler's mountaintop home. Endless switchbacks up a one-lane road through yellowing grass, dry earth. When I finally made it to the top, Maggie greeted me on the deck her husband hadn't been able to enjoy, pollen and dust too dangerous for his sensitive lungs. She led me to the kitchen. After pouring us each a cup of coffee, she told me that it had been hard to watch her husband fall into his researching obsession as he neared the end of his life, spending his time buried in books instead of with her. But she said she thinks he felt a duty to make sure Jane's voice was heard. A duty to unearth a truth that had stayed buried for so long. I asked her if, even though her husband took such pains *not* to accuse David Starr Jordan of murder in the book, he might have privately wondered if David Starr Jordan had been involved.

"He absolutely believed that Jordan did it," she told me, without needing time to think.

"Really?"

"Oh yeah. He thought Jordan was rotten to the core."

The drive back down felt shorter, somehow. I was lost in my thoughts, thinking about my weird attachment to David Starr Jordan, my hope that he was the person who could lead me out of the mess I had made of my life. There was so much I admired about him. His sarcasm. His devotion to the "hidden and insignificant" flowers. His absurd walrus mustache, which reminded me of my dad's clownish push broom. His steel backbone, that gritty resolve that made him refuse to crumple in the face of whatever misfortune came his way. Is this what happens if you employ his sunny disposition? You become so callous, so impervious to obstacles, that you can stomp out a woman's life, or at the very least be willing to cover up the truth of her death?

A retired Stanford archivist whom I called after first hearing about Robert Cutler's book warned me not to be entranced by its theories. She called it "truly not worth talking about," a work of "speculation." "The doctor needed a villain," she said, and urged I pay the book no mind, warning me not to fall prey to a narrative. Historian Luther Spoehr said that Cutler's book convinced him that Jane Stanford had been poisoned, but that to suggest David had ordered it was to cross from speculation to "fantasy."

I finally got myself out to Stanford University's archives, where dozens of David Starr Jordan's boxes of journals, letters, unpublished essays, and drawings lay in wait. I requested the maximum amount of material allowed per day. Morning after morning, I resisted the sunshine beckoning outside the windows, the scent of eucalyptus whispering come-hither. I was searching for some clear admission of guilt in those yellowing pages.

On my fifth day, I came across a folder full of drawings. It was dated just a few years after Jane's death. This time, instead of flowers, it was monsters that David drew. Endless monsters, rendered in that same labored hand. They are wild with color. A lobster with a goat head. A porcupine with rainbow quills. A carnivorous kangaroo dripping magenta blood from her fangs (with a carnivorous baby in her pouch). Dragon after dragon, demon after demon, goat horns galore. They breathe fire; they drip blood; human limbs protrude from their jaws. In one, three squids are choking on their tails. In another, the night sky hemorrhages sharks and wolves and snakes. In another, there is a man with a walrus mustache. He is standing at the back of a crowd, looking off to his side at a woman wearing a floral hat. This man, this one man in a crowd of many, is the sole figure who sports a pair of devil's horns. They are sketched faintly above his head as though they have just filled in.

Deep at the bottom of a box jangling with odds and ends I found a small rectangular notecard. It was from Jane Stanford's brother Charles, thanking David for the condolence flowers he sent after Jane's death. I pictured David reading the card, his thumb pressing into the very same cardstock, and I felt a little shock of disgust. I came across a carefully cut-out newspaper article, folded in half so its contents were hidden from view, titled "Dr. Jordan's Statement Is Riddled by the Experts." In it, the reporter refutes David's explanation of death by natural causes, showing item by item how the evidence points to a poisoning. The article concludes by suggesting that David Starr Jordan must be "covering up a crime" and warns that the killer is still on the loose.

Was the archivist right? I wondered as I flipped through thousands of pages, remnants of David's skin entering my nostrils. Was I doing exactly what I was beginning to suspect David of, twisting the facts to keep my worldview intact, to confirm my daddy's belief that confidence corrupts?

Despite my mounting suspicion of David, I forced myself to encounter his good side, to breathe it in. I carefully read the handwritten remembrance by Jessie calling David the "miracle" of her life. His many poems, odes to the *hidden and insignificant* of this world, sea sponges and sea stars and even grass itself. I read about his tireless work protecting the fur seal from overhunting; I handled the heavy, engraved medallions he won for advocating peace—his passion in later years. I read the article he wrote called "Where Uncle Sam's Solar Plexus Is Located," in which he argues that America's most vulnerable spot was its hub of weapons manufacturing in the mid-Atlantic. A nation too reliant on "the killing business," he wrote, was "in a bad way." Its potential for growth, on the other hand, he claimed

lay in its "public school. . . . It teaches the lesson of personal useful-
ness, of friendship across race lines, of equality before law . . . this is
his source of power." I sniffed his journals, the small leather ones
he carried around in his breast pocket as a young abolitionist; they
smelled of warmed butter. They spilled forth drawings of caterpillars,
spiders, leaves.

I went home empty-handed.

I went home lost, as ever.

It was a couple of months later that I came across the detail that
would send a flash of heat up my neck. I was back in Chicago, still
searching for answers, this time in a copy of one of David Starr
Jordan's fish-collecting manuals, *A Guide to the Study of Fishes*. I had
smiled through his friendly introduction, in which he promised his
readers that fish can be found anywhere, "the old 'swimming hole'
or the deep eddy at the root of the old stump." I flipped through his
diagrams of jawbones, pectoral fins, air bladders. And then, on page
430, I saw it. Under a section called "How to Secure Fishes," he di-
vulges a secret to his intrepid readers, the ones who have stayed with
him this long. His favorite trick for catching the peskiest of fish,
the ones that evade capture by darting into the cracks of tide pools?
Poison. The particular variety he recommends? A dangerous and
powerful substance, one he once described as "the bitterest thing in
the world." Strychnine.

10.

A Veritable Chamber of Horrors

T he erosion of David Starr Jordan's presidential power began almost immediately after Jane Stanford's death. Displeased by his rash dismissal of Jane's informant, Julius Goebel, the board of trustees voted to strip David of his authority to fire faculty. And a few years later, in 1913, the board asked him to step down altogether. They allowed him to keep the ceremonial title of chancellor but divested him of any remaining executive power.

With a heaping amount of free time suddenly on his plate, David found himself a new hobby. His travels as a fish collector had taken him a few times to a village in the Italian Alps called Aosta. There, he had seen something shocking. Aosta was a sort of sanctuary city for people with disabilities, both mental and physical. For centuries, the Catholic Church had provided shelter, food, and care to people who had been rejected by their families because of their condition. And many of these people had ended up becoming skilled workers, in the fields or in kitchens; many of them ended up falling in love, getting married, having children. What had emerged was a sort of upside-down town. A town where the abnormal was normal, where people often disabled by society received the support that allowed them to flourish.

Some might see something beautiful in this town, a radically humane way of helping society's most vulnerable live with dignity.

But David Starr Jordan, when he visited in the 1880s, had described it as "a veritable chamber of horrors," overrun with "creatures" with "less intelligence than the goose . . . less decency than the pig."

Over the years, the town of Aosta continued to nag at David. He worried that it was proof of that thing Louis Agassiz had suggested could take place in the animal world: degeneration. David wrongly believed that immobile creatures like sea squirts and barnacles had once been higher forms of fish and crabs but had "degenerated" back into lazier, weaker, less complex, less intelligent forms of life, as a result of acquiring resources parasitically. More broadly, he believed that any kind of long-term aid to a creature would result in its eventual physical and cognitive decline. He called this misunderstanding of how nature works "animal pauperism," and he worried that the same phenomenon was taking place in Aosta, that the people of Aosta were literally degenerating into a "new species of man." So he began working on a book. A book that would alert the public to the dangers of charity, causing, as he believed it did, "the survival of the unfittest." A book that would recommend the extermination of these "*crétins*" as the only way to prevent against a worldwide "decay" of the human race. A book that would rely heavily on a word that had come into being only a few decades earlier. A word without much popularity in America when he first began. A word he himself would champion with so much zeal and scientific authority, he'd help propagate it on US soil.

Eugenics.

The word was coined back in 1883 by a British scientist named Francis Galton, a famous polymath in his own right, who also happened to be the half cousin of Charles Darwin. When *On the Origin of Species* had first come out, Galton had read his cousin's book and been so inspired he called it a new "epoch in my own mental development." Once Galton had come to comprehend that there were forces of natural selection shaping the array of life on Earth, it dawned on him that perhaps you could actually manipulate those forces to select for a master race of humans, by breeding out traits he incorrectly believed to be associated with blood: poverty, criminality, illiteracy, "feeblemindedness," promiscuity, and more. He called this technique of killing off groups of people you don't like "eugenics," Greek for "good" and "birth." And he began telling anyone who would listen to him—Darwin's cousin!—about his scientific-sounding plan for making Europe great again.

He trotted out his ideas at fancy gatherings and in fancy magazines like *Nature* and *Macmillan's*. He even wrote a sci-fi novel called *The Eugenic College of Kantsaywhere*, about a community where only those who passed rigorous tests were allowed to procreate, and anyone else who tried would be imprisoned and punished with "sharp severity." Galton saw his book as a happy tale. A how-to guide for saving the human race from decay.

Plenty of people dismissed Galton. There's a chance that eugenics could have remained in the realm of speculative fiction had a small group of influential scientists not championed its cause so zealously. David Starr Jordan, despite all his railing against the dangers of "sciosophy," was one of the earliest and loudest. He drank the eugenics Kool-Aid hard and fast. He began hallucinating evidence of heritable personality traits everywhere. Even his smitten biographer, Edward McNall Burns, had to admit it was ludicrous. "He attached so exaggerated an importance to biological inheritance, that he seemed to think almost every quality of human personality could be explained thereby." Poverty, laziness, the ability to classify birds—all simply a matter of the blood!

David Starr Jordan was one of the first to bring Galton's ideas back to America. As early as the 1880s, decades before most American eugenicists got the fever, David had begun to tuck these ideas into his lectures at Indiana University, informing students that traits like "pauperism" and "degener[acy]" were heritable and thus could be "exterminated just as swamps are drained." In time, he began taking the ideas outside of the classroom, giving speeches to large gatherings of prominent politicians warning that the "republic shall endure [only] as long as the human harvest is good." He published his first pro-eugenics article in 1898 and followed it with a flurry of books advocating for the cleansing of the gene pool: *The Human Harvest, The Blood of the Nation, Your Family Tree*, and so on. In his writings, David took all the kinds of people he wanted to rid from the Earth—the paupers and drinkers and "*crétins*" and "imbeciles" and "idiots" and morally depraved—and he lumped them into one category, the "unfit." *Unfit!* Such a catchy word, so evocative, so trim. It could take his opinions about which groups of people deserved to live and wrap them in the cloak of science. *Unfit!* Not one man's judgment, just a reality of nature.

On speaking tours, David made stops at churches and alms-houses, where he'd warn the devoted staffs about the dangers of their work fomenting, as he claimed it did, "the survival of the unfit." He'd share the cautionary tale of Aosta, describing a land where "goitered" and "imbecile" "creatures" roamed free, drooling, panhandling, behaving indecently; an old woman, he claimed, once "even lick[ed] my hands like a dog." He had sketches made of the people he had supposedly met there—an old woman hunched over a cane, grimacing maniacally, with missing teeth and warts; a man with a coconut-size goiter sprouting from his neck—and he warned that this was where the human race was headed if society didn't take action. The solution? Some eugenicists considered paying elites to have more babies to flood the gene pool with "superior" stock. Others suggested legalizing polygamy for the upper class. But David Starr Jordan had what he considered a far better idea. A way of making real that "extermina[tion]" he had once proposed to his students. By simply snipping the reproductive organs of people he saw as "unfit," David assured audiences that "each individual cretin should be the last of his generation."

In the wake of these talks and similar ones given by other early eugenicists, back-alley sterilizations and, occasionally, executions began taking place all over America. In 1915, a doctor in Chicago named Harry Haiselden began leaving disabled babies to die, earning him the nickname "the Black Stork." There were rumors of a mental hospital in Illinois that was intentionally killing off its patients with tuberculosis-infected milk. According to scholar Paul Lombardo, who has done heroic work unearthing huge chunks of this history, a handful of doctors began boasting of sterilizing "unfit" patients, while countless more performed the operation in what was sometimes called the "quiet way"—behind the scenes and without legal authority.

But David Starr Jordan, good Puritan, was not a fan of breaking the law, so he began advocating for the legalization of eugenic sterilization. In 1907, a few of his friends from Bloomington successfully legalized forced eugenic sterilization in Indiana—the first such law not just in the country but in the world. Two years later, David helped get it passed in California. His commitment to the cause apparent, he was asked to chair the Eugenics Committee of the American Breeders Association. He eagerly accepted.

I can't believe I made it through my entire education without ever learning about our country's leading role in the eugenics movement. But eugenics seemed as roaring a part of American culture as flappers and the Model T. This was not a fringe movement; it crossed party lines; the first five presidents of the twentieth century hailed its promise; eugenics courses were taught at prestigious universities all across the country, from Harvard to Stanford to Yale to UC Berkeley to Princeton and back again. There were eugenics magazines. Eugenics cosmetics. Even eugenics competitions. Often held at state fairs, under festive white tents. Contests would be held for the fittest families and best babies—measured and weighed like pumpkins. Blue ribbons for the fairest skin, the roundest head, the most symmetrical features.

And as for the losers? Slowly, more and more states passed sterilization laws. Connecticut. Iowa. New Jersey. Have a sexually transmitted disease? *Snip.* An epileptic seizure? *Snip.* An out-of-wedlock baby, a criminal record, a low score on a standardized test? *Snip. Snip. Snip.*

Still, the actual rate of sterilization was low. The policies David helped to put in place required an "unfit" person to first come into contact with the law or the medical, education, or welfare system before a sterilization could take place. Then, in 1916, an American eugenicist named Madison Grant published a book that a German guy named Hitler would later call his "bible." In the book, *The Passing of the Great Race*, Grant proposed a policy that, in certain ways, resembled Galton's sci-fi vision: that all the nation's "moral perverts, mental defectives and hereditary cripples" be rounded up under the guise of charity and sterilized. American eugenicists thought it was brilliant. When over a decade later Hitler passed Germany's first mandatory sterilization law, American eugenicist and doctor Joseph DeJarnette whined, "The Germans are beating us at our own game."

Not all Americans, however, were so gung-ho about this plan of creating a better society via genetic cleansing. There were some very loud voices of dissent. In 1910, the president of the American Bar Association called eugenic sterilization "barbari[c]"; a lawyer with Oregon's Anti-Sterilization League called it "an engine of tyranny and oppression"; the Catholic Church was one of its loudest opponents, on the grounds that it violated the sanctity of life. In 1906, Pennsylvania governor Samuel Pennypacker struck down what would have been the first compulsory sterilization law in the world, saying, "To permit such an operation would be to inflict cruelty upon a helpless class . . . which the state has undertaken to protect."

And then there was the mounting scientific dissent. More and more scholars were calling the science behind eugenics "rot," pointing out that a person's environment played a crucial role in many of the traits eugenicists thought could be eradicated by sterilization—poverty, promiscuity, illiteracy, criminality. Other scientists questioned the validity of the concept of "degeneration," the idea that charity causes physical deterioration; they were unconvinced that life moved "backwards" in the way David claimed it did, unconvinced that sea squirts, for example, had devolved into immobile sacs as a result of relying on food from other species. These skeptics would later be proved right.

And then there was that key point in *On the Origin of Species.* That crucial point that somehow both David and before him Francis Galton had missed. What does Darwin say is the best way of building a strong species, of allowing it to endure into the future, to withstand the blows of Chaos in all her mighty forms—flood, drought, rising sea levels, fluctuating temperatures, invasions of competitors, predators, pests?

Variation. Variation in genes, and hence in behavior and physical traits. Homogeneity is a death sentence. To rid a species of its mutants and outliers is to make that species dangerously vulnerable to the elements. In nearly every chapter of *Origin*, Darwin hails the power of "Variation." He marvels over how diverse gene pools are healthier and stronger, how intercrossing between different types of individuals gives more "vigor and fertility" to their offspring, how even worms and plants that can produce perfect replicas of themselves are equipped for sex, for introducing variety back into the gene pool. "How strange are these facts!" he cries. "How simply are these facts explained on the view of an occasional cross with a distinct individual being advantageous or indispensable!"

"Diversify your genetic portfolio" would be another way of saying it. You never know which traits could prove useful as conditions change. Darwin even goes out of his way to warn against meddling. The danger, as he sees it, is the fallibility of the human eye, our inability to comprehend complexity. Traits that might seem "abhorrent to our ideas of fitness" could actually be beneficial to a species or ecosystem, or could, in time, become beneficial as conditions change. It was that ungainly neck that gave the giraffe an edge over its competitors, the seeming deadweight of blubber that allowed the seal to thrive in the advancing cold, the divergent human brain that might hold the key to inventions, discoveries, and revolutions that the majority is unable to fathom. "Man can act only on external and visible characters; nature cares nothing for appearances. . . . She can act on every internal organ, on every shade of constitutional difference, on the whole machinery of life."

Consider the case of the cyanobacteria. A tiny green speck in the sea, so insignificant to the human eye that for centuries we didn't even have a name for it. Until one day in the 1980s when scientists accidentally discovered it was producing a significant portion of the oxygen we breathe. Now we revere it, this tiny green speck, *Prochlorococcus marinus*; we fight to protect it. This was the kind of scenario Darwin prophesied. Why he warned, so unambiguously, against attempting to rank Earth's bounty: "Which group will prevail, no man can predict."

And this wariness, this humility, this reverence for an ecological complexity that defies human comprehension is, in fact, a very old idea. It's a basic philosophical concept sometimes called the "dandelion principle": in some contexts a dandelion might be considered a weed to be culled; in others, it's a valuable medicinal herb to be cultivated.

The eugenicists failed to consider this very simple principle of relativity. By trying to cull the gene pool of its "indispensable" variety, they were in fact foiling their very best shot of building a master race.

And yet not a single one of these arguments, philosophical, moral, or scientific, seemed to penetrate David's certainty about eugenics. He, along with other eugenicists, dismissed their dissenters as naïve, sentimental, too dim to see the bigger picture. "[E]ducation can never replace heredity," David declared in a eugenics manifesto entitled *Your Family Tree*, adding: "An Arab proverb puts the matter bluntly: 'Father a weed; mother a weed; do you expect daughter to be a saffron root?'"

In fact, in the face of mounting dissent, David only pushed harder to create a mandatory eugenics program in America. He persuaded his friend the wealthy widow Mary Harriman to give over half a million dollars (about $13 million today) to seed the Eugenics Record Office, a shiny, new pro-eugenics research hub in Cold Spring Harbor, New York. The ERO would go on to collect boatloads of data on tens of thousands of Americans. The researchers would then use the information to construct family trees that suggested that complicated phenomena such as poverty, criminality, promiscuity, dishonesty, and a fondness for the ocean (which was given the clinical term "thalassophilia") were predestined in the blood. While the ERO did turn up a few legitimate discoveries—useful information about the inheritance of albinism and neurofibromatosis, for example—the majority of its work would be unequivocally debunked. The researchers had a habit of fudging data, of encoding gossip as fact, and it is now well established that intergenerational poverty or criminality, for example, is brought about by a swirl of insidious environmental factors.

In spite of the studies churned out by the prestigious ERO (it also received substantial support from the Rockefeller family and the Carnegie Institution), by the early 1920s the public was beginning to change its tune on the subject. More and more doctors who had performed sterilizations faced lawsuits, and the Supreme Court of New Jersey decided to strike down its eugenic sterilization law due to its "palpable inhumanity and immorality." It was looking like perhaps David's dream of a national eugenics program had finally fizzled out.

Enter Albert Priddy.

Priddy was the slick-haired doctor in charge of the Virginia State Colony for Epileptics and Feebleminded, in Lynchburg, Virginia. He was a zealous eugenicist, known for having sterilized women for being "man-crazy," having "wanderlust," telling "coarse stories," and even passing notes in class. In 1917, he had been sued by a man named George Mallory for sterilizing his wife and daughter while Mallory had been traveling for work. Dr. Priddy's justification? That a house full of women with no man in charge must have been a brothel.

"I am a humanbeen as well as you," Mallory wrote to Priddy after learning what Priddy had done. "You ought be ashamed of your selft. . . . Just stop and think of how she have been treated." The judge sided with Priddy, but the Colony was shaken by the lawsuit and urged Priddy to cool it on the sterilizations. Instead of repenting, though, Dr. Priddy dug in. He began searching for a case that would prove to juries that "feeblemindedness" was hereditary and must be stopped by sterilization.

And one day in 1924, Dr. Priddy found what he'd been looking for. A young woman named Carrie Buck was dropped off at the Colony. She was an orphan, and had become pregnant at the age of seventeen after being raped. After she gave birth, her foster parents sent her away to the Colony. When Carrie landed on Dr. Priddy's doorstep, he was struck by something familiar about her face. Those high cheekbones, those pensive eyes. It turned out that her biological mother, Emma Buck, was also in residence at the Colony under allegations of being a prostitute. After Priddy realized the two women were related, he had Carrie's baby, Vivian, tested by a famous eugenicist researcher from the ERO. The researcher ran a few tests—likely running a coin in front of the baby's eyes or clapping his hands to test her attention—and determined that little Vivian "showed backwardness." This official assessment then gave Priddy the thing he had been dreaming of for years. Proof that "feeblemindedness" was heritable over three generations.

A lawyer named Irving Whitehead was appointed to represent Carrie Buck to protest sterilization, but scholarship by Lombardo suggests that Whitehead was a proponent of eugenic sterilization, likely in cahoots with Dr. Priddy. When the prosecution accused Carrie of coming from a "shiftless, ignorant, and worthless class of people," Whitehead failed to provide what could have been a decent defense for Buck (she had good school records, and neighbors and teachers willing to vouch for her integrity) and kept appealing the ruling until he got all the way to the Supreme Court.

The year was 1927. The month was April. David Starr Jordan was seventy-six years old. He had begun to grow weak. Just a year earlier, his son Eric—little Eric, his replacement for Barbara, this boy who had grown into a paleontologist—had died in a car accident at the age twenty-two as he headed out on a collecting trip. David was weak from grief, weak from exhaustion, weak from too many years of formaldehyde eating away at his eyes; his vision was going; he had developed diabetes; in just a couple of years he would need a wheelchair. But he would have been energized by the reports pouring through his radio. Scientists from the ERO, an institution that he had helped bring into existence, were providing evidence to the Supreme Court, asserting that "moral delinquency" was encoded in the blood and could be eliminated through mandatory sterilization. This notion that had once been a hazy idea in David's mind had, through his proselytizing, become a thing of this Earth. An entity so real it was poised on the precipice of entering federal law.

The nine somber-faced justices considered the evidence, the fancy words and intricate family trees that suggested sterilization was a sound way of protecting citizens against crime, illness, poverty, suffering. They considered the girl, Carrie: timid and trusting. Asked during her first hearing if she had anything to say for herself, she had replied, "No, sir, I have not. . . . It is up to my people." Her people voted 8 to 1 to make compulsory sterilizations legal "in order to prevent our being swamped with incompetence."

Five months later, Carrie Buck was taken into a squat brick building at the Lynchburg Colony and brought to the second floor, where a skylight provided extra light for the surgeon. She was placed on an operating table and sliced open just above her pubis. Using probes, the surgeon located her fallopian tubes and swiftly ligated each one. He then sealed each cut with carbolic acid so the dead end would hold tight.

Carrie awoke to a new reality: that no other child with her distinctive eyes, with her unique mix of traits, would ever walk this Earth again. "They done me wrong," she would later say. "They done us all wrong."

Carrie's case paved the way for over 60,000 sterilizations, performed legally and against people's will, all over America in the name of "public welfare." Many of the "unfit" have been forgotten, but researchers have fought to keep what stories they can find in the light. In 2007, a historian from the University of Michigan, Alexandra Minna Stern, discovered a set of microfilm reels in an old file cabinet in a government office in Sacramento. On them was a sort of eugenics registry—the names and demographic information of every person sterilized in David's adopted home of California from 1919 to 1952. The list was nearly 20,000 people long.

Stern has spent years analyzing the records with a team, and together they've been able to fill in the picture of what "unfit" really meant, what kinds of people lived inside that category. As Stern writes, those deemed unfit were "often were young women pronounced promiscuous; the sons and daughters of Mexican, Italian, and Japanese immigrants . . . and men and women who transgressed sexual norms." Other studies have shown how women of color were disproportionately targeted for sterilization. The US government has admitted to forcefully sterilizing over 2,500 Native American women in the early 1970s. The Eugenics Board of North Carolina sought out and sterilized hundreds of black women during the 1960s and 1970s. And, mind bogglingly, approximately *a third* of all Puerto Rican women were sterilized by the US government between 1933 and 1968.

The ruling that made this all possible, by the way, is still on the books. That's right. The Supreme Court ruling has never been overturned. At our highest level, it is still written into law that if the government deems you "unfit," officials have the authority to pull you from your home, stick a knife through your abdomen, and terminate your bloodline.

While most legal scholars will tell you that *technically* the law is in a state of limbo because every state has since repealed its eugenic sterilization law, the reality is that nearly half of the states still allow for involuntary sterilization of people deemed unfit, only now they use words like "mentally incompetent" or "mentally deficient." Meanwhile, forced sterilization continues to be performed in the "quiet way" all over the country. Much of it remains undocumented and hard to catch—coercive sterilizations in low-income hospitals, meth clinics, prisons, institutions for people with disabilities, and beyond—but big cases come to light every few years. Over the period of 2006 to 2010, for example, nearly 150 women were illegally sterilized in California prisons, without the women's consent and occasionally without their knowledge. And in the summer of 2017, a Tennessee judge named Sam Benningfield was found to be offering petty criminals reduced jail sentences in exchange for being sterilized.

There it is. That same mind-set. Galton's folly. The misbelief that poverty and suffering and criminality are a matter of the blood and can be excised from society with a knife. Eugenic ideology is anything but dead in this country; we are sticky with the stuff.

Stroll down the National Mall in Washington, and when you get to Twenty-First Street, look north and you will see him. Francis Galton, in bronze, over the doorway to our nation's temple to science, the National Academy of Sciences. Walk up the main promenade on Stanford's campus, and one of the first statues to greet you is that of Louis Agassiz, believer that blacks are subhuman, still presiding from his Corinthian pilaster. Behind him is a massive sandstone building, with sweeping archways and a clay tile roof, named in honor of the man who toured our country calling for the "exterminat[ion]" of society's most vulnerable groups. Jordan Hall.

11.

The Ladder

avid Starr Jordan remained an ardent eugenicist until his dying day. There's no evidence of any last-moment realization or remorse. Not about the thousands of people who were brandished with scars and shame thanks to his efforts. Not about the individuals he trampled as he fought to maintain his power—Jane Stanford, the doctors he slandered, the spy he fired, the librarian he accused of sexual perversity.

It was chilling. His brutality. His remorselessness. The sheer depth of his descent, the breadth of his rampage. I felt sick. I had been fashioning myself after a villain, after all. A man so sure of himself and his ideas that he was capable of ignoring reason, of ignoring morality, of ignoring the clamor of thousands of people begging him to see the error of his ways—*I am a humanbeen as well as you.*

How had it happened?

How had that sweet boy, so devoted to caring for the "hidden and insignificant," turned into a man who would so readily kill off the same? Where in his story had he changed? And why?

Looking at the full spread of David's emotional anatomy, the most obvious culprit seems to be that thick "shield of optimism" he was so proud to possess. He had "a terrifying capacity for convincing himself that what he wanted was right," writes scholar Luther

Spoehr, who was struck by how David's certainty in himself, his self-delusion and hardheadedness, only seemed to intensify over the years. "His ability to crush those in his path multiplied even as he became convinced that his path was the one of righteousness which led to progress." As much as David had railed publicly against self-delusion, *privately* he seemed to rely on it, especially in times of trial. *It is the will of man that shapes the fates.* Perhaps that group of psychologists had been right, the ones who warned that positive illusions can ferment into a vicious thing if left unchecked, capable of striking out against anything that stands in our way.

But could that have explained all of it? How hard David was able to push his eugenics agenda, how far? Overconfidence, grit, and pride make a dangerous cocktail, surely, but they didn't seem to fully account for how rabidly he devoted himself to the cause of genetic cleansing.

I worked backward, looking for the swerve, the event or idea that nudged his rudder, made him veer so disastrously off course. I scanned back through the chapters of his life, the boat trips across the Pacific, the Garden of Eden in Palo Alto, the fire in Bloomington, the starry nights of his boyhood in upstate New York. Year by year, I went, sifting through his stories, unstacking the encounters, jar by jar, fish by fish.

Until, eventually, I found myself inside a barn on Penikese Island, beneath a halo of circling swallows, examining the germ of an idea that Louis Agassiz had implanted in young David's mind. It was the belief that there is a ladder built into nature. A *Scala Naturae.* A divine hierarchy from bacteria to humans that points objectively toward better.

This idea rebuilt David's world. It transformed his shameful habit of collecting flowers into "missionary work of the highest order." It filled the cavity of his chest with a burst of purpose that sailed him through life, winning him jobs, awards, wives, children, presidencies.

It fueled his work, through one disaster and then the next. Onward he went, reading nature like a compass, believing that in the shape of a fin or a skull lay moral guidance. He was sure that if he looked closely enough he could glean whom to emulate and whom to condemn; he could glean, in short, the true path to enlightenment, to peace, to whatever fruits lay at the top of that ladder.

And when he thought he saw humanity beginning to slip, he felt called to rescue it by any means necessary. He wielded his belief in a natural order like a blade, convincing people that sterilization was the soundest way—the only way—of saving the human race.

"I just wish he had considered what Oliver Cromwell once said," Luther Spoehr told me on the phone one June morning, as he tried to make sense of this man he had studied for so many years. "'I beseech thee in the bowels of Christ, consider that thee might be mistaken.'"

"Are you saying you wish he had more doubt?" I asked.

"Yup."

But he didn't. Despite his prophet's warning—that "science, generally, hates beliefs"—David held fast to this idea of a ladder. He clung to it, in the face of waves of counterevidence that should have eventually eroded it.

When Darwin came along, debunking the idea of a divine plan, David accepted that Earth's creatures had come about accidentally. But he somehow found a way to preserve the idea of a hierarchy of perfection. He told himself that time, not God, had forged its shape—the slow tick of time forming fitter, more intelligent, more morally advanced forms of life.

When he encountered the growing chorus of opposition to his eugenics agenda, when judges and lawyers and governors began trying to overturn eugenic laws, he wrote them off as sentimental, unscientific. When *scientists* began to question eugenics, to point out all its shoddy assumptions about the heritability of morality, about the concept of degeneration, he questioned their courage, their commitment to the cause of bettering society.

But perhaps the most damning argument came from nature herself. Had David followed his own advice to look to nature for truth, he would have seen it. This dazzling, feathery, squawking, gurgling mound of counterevidence. Animals can outperform humans on nearly every measure supposedly associated with our superiority. There are crows that have better memories than us, chimps with better pattern-recognition skills, ants that rescue their wounded, and blood flukes with higher rates of monogamy. When you actually examine the range of life on Earth, it takes a lot of acrobatics to sort it into a single hierarchy with humans at the top. We don't have the biggest brain or the best memory. We're not the fastest or the strongest or the most prolific. We're not the only ones that mate for life, that show altruism, use tools, language. We don't have the most copies of genes in circulation. We aren't even the newest creation on the block.

This was what Darwin was trying so hard to get his readers to see. There is no ladder. *Natura non facit saltum*, he cries in his scientist's tongue. There are no "jumps." The rungs we see are figments of our imagination, more about "convenience" than truth. To Darwin, a parasite was not an abomination but a marvel. A case of extraordinary adaptability. The sheer range of creatures in existence, great and small, feathered and glowing, goitered and smooth, was *proof* that there are endless ways of surviving and thriving in this world.

So why was David unable to see it? This mountain of counterevidence stacked up against his faith in a ladder. Why would he protect it, this arbitrary belief about how plants and creatures should be arranged? When challenged, why would he only double down and use it to justify such violent measures?

Perhaps because his belief gave him something more important than truth.

Not just that first spark of purpose as a young man on Penikese, not just a career and a cause and a wife and a cushy life. But something even more profound. A way of turning that roiling morass, of the sea, of the stars, of his dizzying life, into clear, shining order.

To let go, at any point—from his first read of Darwin to his last push for eugenics—would have been to invite a return to vertigo. He would have been transported back to being that lost little boy, shaking before a world that had just taken his brother. A terrified child, powerless before the world, with no way of understanding or controlling it. To let go of that hierarchy would be to release a tornado of life, beetles and hawks and bacteria and sharks, swirling high into the air, all around him, above him.

It would have been too disorienting.

It would have been Chaos.

It would have been—

—the very same vision of the world I myself had been fighting so hard not to look at ever since I was a little girl. That sense of falling off the edge of the world, plummeting alongside ants and stars, with no purpose or point. Of glimpsing the glaring, relentless truth so clear from inside the swirl of Chaos. *You don't matter.*

That's what the ladder offered David. An antidote. A foothold. The lovely, warm feeling of significance.

In that light, I could understand why he clung to it so tightly, this vision of a natural order. Why he protected it so ferociously—against morality, against reason, against truth. Even as I despised him for it, on some level I craved the very same thing.

I closed David Starr Jordan's autobiography. The second and final olive-green volume. I set it on the nightstand in my little guest room in Heather's apartment in Chicago. The night air was quiet.

Heather was staying across the city with her boyfriend. The hot light of the city screamed through the window.

There were a few stars. They were hard to see, but they were there, winking behind the pink garbage mess we have made of the sky. I was back on the earth I had been trying so hard to escape. The bleak one, with no refuge or promises no matter what you do, how much you believe in your mission, or how hard you repent. I had made a wreck of my life. And I wasn't going to lie to myself any longer. The curly-haired man was never coming back. David Starr Jordan wasn't going to lead me into some beautiful new existence. There was no way of overcoming Chaos, no guide or shortcut or magic phrase to guarantee everything would end up okay.

So what do you do after letting go of hope? Where do you go?

12.

Dandelions

 he road to Lynchburg is flanked by end-
less gun stores. Even the gas stations sell
them. *New Glock Pistols!!*, they say. *Shoot-
ing Range! 25% Off Ammo!* I was driving
to the Virginia State Colony for Epilep-
tics and Feebleminded. That fenced internment camp where David's wildest ideas had transmuted into reality, where thousands had
been segregated from society, imprisoned, and sterilized.

After crossing the James River, I turned right onto Colony Road,
a one-lane paved road about a mile long. Just before the entrance
to the Colony there is a gravel pull-off, where you can behold the
Blue Ridge Mountains, rolling like lavender waves, just out of reach.

When I came to the gates, I discovered there are no longer any
gates. Just a large brick embankment off to one side, as if to remind
motorists of the boundary that used to reign. A sign informed me
that this was a Tobacco-Free Facility, that it was now called the
Central Virginia Training Center. I was shocked to learn that people with disabilities still lived here, that it still operated as a state-
run care facility. It would close its doors a few years after I visited,
though, when living conditions were found to be inadequate.

The campus was even larger than I had imagined. Sprawling,
with over sixty buildings, hundreds of acres. I parked my car in
front of a foreboding brick building, four stories tall, with a white

tower and a massive set of stairs leading to an entrance supported by six white columns. This was the main building, where so many people had once been processed, examined, deemed unfit to carry on their genetic lines. The only other vehicle in the lot was a police car, parked over two spots. I wasn't sure if I was allowed to be here. Tentatively, I got out of my car.

I began walking the paths. I walked by dozens of hulking brick buildings with black mold creeping up their sides. They were all abandoned. The functional part of the facility was located down the hill a bit, away from these grisly relics of the past. I walked by the remnants of a barn and field where the inmates had been forced to tend cows, hogs, and various crops at a profit to the Colony. I walked by a gazebo, a swing set, a cemetery. Turkey buzzards circled in what seemed like an enlarged sky.

I walked through the cemetery gates and discovered over a thousand graves. Emma Bishop. Eighteen years old. Dorothy Mitchell. Twelve years old. Alfred Snyder. Three years old. Each gravestone was a small flat rectangle, flush with the dirt.

I kept walking. I had the chilling thought that this faraway, desolate hilltop was ground zero for eugenic extermination. The very mind-set we define our national identity in opposition to—the evil that we tell our schoolchildren started with the Nazis, the others, the bad guys—we were the first in the world to make it national policy.

Finally, I made it to the building where Carrie Buck was sterilized. It was a squat brick box with rotting edges. The floorboards on its porch were falling out. A drainpipe had rusted off. There was a chain obstructing its steps. DANGER: DO NOT ENTER. Below the porch, a basement window was open. I crawled over to it and peered inside to see a series of sunken rooms with dilapidated walls. A cold rush of air smacked me in the face. I looked upward, to a window on the top floor. Four of its panes of glass were punched out. A white curtain billowed in the breeze, not realizing there was no one left inside to protect from the sun, to soothe, to hide.

I would never be able to ask Carrie Buck about what happened to her here. She died in 1983, in a nursing home in Virginia. Her daughter, Vivian, had died decades earlier at the age of eight due to complications from the measles. Shortly after making honor roll at the local elementary school.

But eventually, after months of searching, I was able to find a woman who knew these Colony grounds all too well, who had spent the majority of her childhood locked inside them. Her name is Anna, and she looks like she could be friends with your mom. Short gray haircut, floral blouse, carrying a purse.

The first time I met her, we convened at a Dairy Queen. We both got vanilla ice cream cones, dipped in chocolate. She told me that underneath her blouse there is a large scar that runs vertically up her abdomen. It is purple and gnarled in some spots. She says she does her best not to look at it—in the shower, in the mirror, as she is getting dressed in the morning. "I think about it every day, though."

She was sterilized against her will at the Lynchburg facility when she was nineteen years old. The year was 1967. But she had first landed inside its brick walls twelve years earlier, when she was just seven years old. She and her brothers had been spotted by neighbors playing naked and unattended in a pen behind their home. State workers had come to take them away. It didn't matter that the kids didn't want to go. Anna loved her mom, her long hair and overalls, how she'd let Anna climb into bed with her when the nights were cold. But the combination of the neighbors' worries, her parents' poverty, and Anna's low score on an intelligence test were enough to deem this seven-year-old "unfit." A threat to humankind.

Anna remembers being driven, in a patrol car of some sort, up that long, narrow road toward the Colony on its hill, a gate opening, a guard waving them through. She and her brothers were marched up big steps into a foreboding brick building. She had no idea why they were there.

They did not sterilize her right away. First she was made to cut her long hair, then she was issued an inmate number, and finally she was made to wait. Year after year, to wait, while an alternate childhood roamed free just outside those gates, through the blue-ridged silhouettes in the distance.

She said that they were treated like animals in the Colony, corralled into large sleeping quarters, forced to work with no pay, made to line up outside as they waited for meals, even if it was raining, even if it was sleeting. If they disobeyed, they were put in "the blind room." There were no lights in the blind room, no windows. They were left in the dark, sometimes for days, without food or water or a toilet. She remembers the urine pooling beneath her bare feet. She is shy when she tells me about being raped. Not in the blind room, no. In her psychologist's office. He closed the door and tied her legs to the examining table.

Anna was told that if she wanted to leave the Colony, it was easy. Just agree to be sterilized, they said, and she would be free. But little Anna refused. She'd heard about people dying on the operating table. She'd watched the little cemetery slowly fill with more and more gravestones.

Plus, she wanted to have kids. Kids were her only dream. She wanted to build a busy home full of laughter and warmth. She knew she could do it. And her keepers must have known it, too, on some level, because Anna's job in the Colony was to care for other inmates—to bathe them, sing to them, help them into their pajamas, rock them to sleep. Fit to care for the state's children, but not her own.

For years, she refused to be sterilized, hoping that someone—her parents, her president, someone somewhere fighting for Good—

would come and set her free. She refused to give her captors the one part of her identity she wanted to keep for herself, Mother. She refused to hand over the one source of hope keeping her going.

One day in the early sixties, a little girl showed up at the Colony. Her name was Mary and she was shaken, afraid, wanting very much to go home. "I told her don't worry, everything will be okay," said Anna. And then thirteen-year-old Anna took little Mary under her wing. She pushed her on the swings, let her cling to her dress as they talked to boys, told her which staff members to avoid, and which had candy. Mary would later tell me that she's not sure how she would have survived her time there without Anna.

Eventually Anna's adolescence gave way to adulthood. With new muscles—of the leg, of the mind—Anna managed to escape over the fence and into the woods. She ran. Down the hill, through the trees, toward the mountains, toward the train tracks, toward anything else. But she was picked up by police before even making it into town. They drove her back to the Colony. The gates closed behind her and she was beaten for having tried—her head pounded into a wall.

Unfit, not a judgment, just a fact of life.

Then, on a muggy August day in 1967, a few months after she'd turned nineteen, a nurse told Anna she had to have a checkup. She led her to an examining room, strapped a mask to her face, and left the room. Anna watched the walls around her start to wave and blur. She figured she was being euthanized. "I thought I was gone. And I wasn't gonna wake up," she told me. "But I woke up."

Wake up, she did. To a bandage on her stomach, twenty-five crudely tied stitches trying to conceal a robbery. No one told her what they had done to her. They just told her that she would soon be free to leave.

Nowadays Anna lives in a two-bedroom apartment just a few miles from where the Colony still looms on its hill. The other occupant of the home is Mary, her close friend from youth. The two have lived together for the past decade or so. After being released from the Lynchburg facility, Mary married Anna's brother Roy. While the marriage didn't last long, Anna and Mary had so loved the feeling of being legal family, sisters-in-law, that they've called themselves sisters ever since.

Anna opens the door when I arrive. Mary is sitting in a La-Z-Boy and waves at me with her cane, beckoning for a hug. I hear birds squawking. The women introduce me to their pair of parakeets, Pretty Boy and Pretty Girl. One yellow, one blue. There is a jungle of plants, ivies and succulents and hanging philodendrons. On the couch, sitting upright in a white onesie and tiny pink sneakers, is a doll. A perfect replica of a human infant, with marble-blue eyes and plastic lips.

Mary gives me a hug. Anna hurries to the kitchen to get me some iced tea. She refills Mary's glass while she's at it. Then she settles into a matching La-Z-Boy next to Mary and tells me how they moved into houses on the same street after making it out of the Colony.

"They told Anna she couldn't take care of kids, but she took care of my kid," Mary says. Mary was able to escape sterilization at the Colony and years later had a son, with her second husband. Anna lived just a few doors down and would come over at the drop of a hat to babysit. "Anytime I needed her, she was always there!"

"He was a sweet baby, he sure was," says Anna. She tells me about taking him to the park, about how he loved to be chased—squealing, then turning back to make sure she was still chasing him. Eventually she trails off. "I always wanted kids, but I couldn't have none."

"Eh," Mary says, swatting the air, quick with a joke about how kids aren't all they're cracked up to be: "I mean, the doctor bills alone . . ."

Anna's shoulders start bouncing, then Mary's go too. The room fills with laughter—Mary's brassy coughs and Anna's softer chuckles. Anna brings out a picture of Mary's son, now a grown man. He has dark hair, a movie-star chin, his arm around a brood of his own children.

"Tell her about *your* baby," Mary says. And Anna finally introduces me to the doll sitting on the couch. "This is Little Mary," she says. She tells me that she brings Little Mary everywhere. To church. To Walmart. Into bed with her each night. She says that a few years ago a freak cyclone destroyed the trailer in which they'd been living. She and (human) Mary had been out that day, but the doll had been trapped under fallen debris. Now she can't bear to ever leave her alone again.

Mary jumps in to say that sometimes Anna gets strange looks for carrying her doll around. Just the other day there was a woman on the bus staring at her. "I told Anna, 'Don't put that baby to the side!' I said, 'Hug her! Don't pay no attention to what people say about your baby. That's *your* baby.'" Anna smiles and gives the doll's bald head a little peck. She taps a doll bottle against its hard lips, dabs away imaginary milk. She draws the doll to her chest, vanishes into the embrace for just a moment, then reappears to bounce her, burp her, thump the cotton of her back.

When I asked Anna what she thought of people like David Starr Jordan, the ones who peddled the ideas that would steal so much away from her—her freedom, her childhood, her dream of having children—she said she felt angry.

But she tries not to focus on the anger, not to look at the scar. Instead, she lives the hell out of the life the eugenicists didn't think she was worthy of living. She drinks her iced tea, ice-cold. She waters her plants. She colors. Page after page of cheerful animals. A surfing fox. A kayaking wolf. A rabbit, a snail, and a butterfly, dancing in a conga line. She saves her scant money to cheer up her friend. After

Mary found out her son and grandkids wouldn't be able to visit for Christmas the past year, Anna rushed out and got her the best present she could think of. A living, breathing, heart-beating hamster. Mary was overcome when she saw it. She named him Sugarfoot and shows me how she greets him each morning, scooping him from his cage and pressing his tiny twitching cheek against hers. You can almost hear a purr. Inside the birdcage, a miniature disco ball turns in the sunlight, throwing dozens of tiny sparkles across the room. Pretty Boy and Pretty Girl flit their wings, as if clapping. The ice cubes in everybody's glasses pop and tinkle as the morning whirls on. The living room is a menagerie of movement and light and laughter and warmth. The living room is alive.

As I drove away from their home that day, I thought about the eugenicists' belief that these lives were not worthy of life. That these lives were somehow a danger to society. It made me furious.

I thought about the gnarled scar on Anna's abdomen. I wondered what it would feel like to look down and see a Supreme Court–sanctioned stamp of unworthiness. To know that the purple ribbon of it had been intended as a gift. The nation's mercy of letting you finish out your years instead of killing you, as they would have wished, on the spot.

I thought about the fact that had David Starr Jordan looked at my sister, he probably would have deemed her unfit. Because she gets flustered at cash registers, okay. I thought about how he likely would have deemed me unfit, too. My sadness repugnant to him, a sign of moral failure. A sulfur-breathed waste of a life.

I wanted to have some amazing retort. Some grandstandy way of telling him how wrong he was. That we matter, we matter. But as soon as I'd feel my fist lifting, my brain would tug it back. Because of course, we don't. We *don't* matter. This is the cold truth of the universe. We are specks, flickering in and out of existence, with no significance to the cosmos. To ignore this truth is, oddly enough, to behave exactly like David Starr Jordan, whose ridiculous belief in his own superiority allowed him to perpetrate such unthinkable violence. No, to be clear-eyed and Good was to concede with every breath, with every step, our insignificance. To say otherwise was to sin, to lie, to march oneself off toward delusion, madness, or worse.

Oh, it was a tangle.

An ouroboros eating its tail.

A blue-tailed skink climbing for redemption only to get smacked down by the truth of the eagle on high.

I felt stuck.

I had asked Anna a stupid question as I sat with her and Mary in their living room that morning. A selfish and indulgent question. After she had told me tales of her internment, of her abuse, of her rape, of being called retarded, of being pushed in the mud, of her jaw being broken, of her reproductive organs being mutilated, I had asked her: "How do you go on?"

It was the question I'd been asking of everyone, in a way, for my whole life. It was the reason I'd spent so many years researching David Starr Jordan's life; it was the question I'd asked my father when I was a little girl; it was why I'd been so reluctant to let go of the curly-haired man, his mesmerizing way of pulling laughter from the cold earth. That levity was the quality I wanted to be near, the substance I wanted to learn how to manufacture in myself, the recipe that, as far and wide as I searched, I seemed unable to find.

Anna looked at me, unsure. She began to think about it. I looked at the plants to give her some space.

Finally, Mary jumped in. "Because of me!"

Anna started laughing. Sure. Right. Of course. "Because of *Mary*."

It was a joke, Mary's way of saving us all from my misstep. But the more I thought back on it, the more I began to wonder about its truth. I thought back on their apartment, the matching La-Z-Boys, the matching parakeets, the matching glasses of iced tea. The doll, propped up on the couch. The hamster whirling in its cage. I started to see this thing I had not consciously noticed as I was sitting there. This sort of invisible thread between the two women. How vigilantly they tend to each other, swatting away the other's sadness, volleying back every joke, laboring to keep the atmosphere light.

All these years later, Anna is still taking care of Mary. It is Anna who answers the door, Anna who fetches Mary a drink, Anna who waters the plants because Mary's knees ache too much to stand. It was Anna who set up Mary with her current boyfriend, Mike. Though Anna is the smaller one now, the more timid one, though she lacks so many of the successes that Mary has come to accrue (the child, the grandchildren, the quick sense of humor, the endless string of romances), Anna is still Mary's protector. She is still pushing her on the proverbial swings, trying to thrill her with whatever humble delights she can tug out of this earth—gravity, iced tea, hamsters.

And Mary. You can see, in nearly every interaction, how grateful she is. She does not judge her friend for loving a doll. Instead, she bolsters that love. Mary pointed to a colorful, beaded necklace hanging around the doll's neck. "I made that!" she said. I pictured Mary, alone in her room, quietly stringing bead after bead up a nylon cord, carefully preparing this surprise for her friend. You get that she is forever repaying the debt of Anna's protection at the Colony. That she finds real meaning in paying it back.

As I kept driving, the sky beginning to plump with darkness, I realized they had shown me evidence of other threads, too, threads that spun out far beyond the walls of that apartment. They had told me about a woman named Gail from their church who stops by a couple of times a month to cook dinner for them, to help with the bills, to chat. They told me about Mary's stepson, Josh, who sends them funny texts nearly every day. About a lawyer named Mark Bold who fought for years to get Anna financial restitution for being sterilized, finally winning her $25,000 and refusing to accept a single cent for his efforts. They told me about their neighbor Grant, who waves at them from his balcony each morning. About the receptionist at their apartment complex, Ebony, whom they call their "guardian angel" because she pulled so many strings to get them into their unit after the cyclone destroyed their trailer. I remembered that when I had checked in at the front desk, Ebony's eyes had lit up when she heard who I was there to see. "Ahhhh," she said, "those are my sweethearts!" She pointed to a series of Anna's drawings taped over her desk. A sleepy puppy. A blushing fox. She said they've been showering her with gratitude since the moment they walked in the door. She says she doesn't deserve it, really, but it's a welcome break in her long, complaint-ridden days.

Slowly, it came into focus. This small web of people keeping one another afloat. All these miniscule interactions—a friendly wave, a pencil sketch, some plastic beads strung up a nylon cord—they might not look like much from the outside, but for the people caught inside that web? They might be everything, the very tethers that keep one bound to this planet.

That was what was so maddening about the eugenicists. They failed to even consider the *possibility* of a web like this. They failed to consider the tangible ways in which people like Anna and Mary might be enriching the society around them, reflecting more light back into it, strengthening it. Mary is not sure she would have survived the Colony without Anna. Well, that. That was something. Was it not? The difference between life and death. Did that not count for something?

And that's when it hit me. That it was not a lie to say that Anna *matters*. Or that Mary matters. Or that—hold on to your seat—you matter, Reader.

It wasn't a lie to say so, but a more accurate way of seeing nature.

It was the *dandelion principle*!

To some people a dandelion might look like a weed, but to others that same plant can be so much more. To an herbalist, it's a medicine—a way of detoxifying the liver, clearing the skin, and strengthening the eyes. To a painter, it's a pigment; to a hippie, a crown; a child, a wish. To a butterfly, it's sustenance; to a bee, a mating bed; to an ant, one point in a vast olfactory atlas.

And so it must be with humans, with *us*. From the perspective of the stars or infinity or some eugenic dream of perfection, sure, one human life might not seem to matter. It might be a speck on a speck on a speck, soon gone. But that was just *one* of infinite perspectives. From the perspective of an apartment in Lynchburg, Virginia, that very same human could be so much more. A stand-in mother. A source of laughter. A way of surviving one's darkest years.

This was what Darwin was trying so hard to get his readers to see: that there is never just one way of ranking nature's organisms. To get stuck on a single hierarchy is to miss the bigger picture, the messy truth of nature, the "whole machinery of life." The work of good science is to try to peer beyond the "convenient" lines we draw over nature. To peer beyond intuition, where something wilder lives. To know that in every organism at which you gaze, there is complexity you will never comprehend.

As I kept driving, I pictured all the dandelions in the whole wide world nodding their heads in unison at me finally getting it, waving beyond my wheels, shaking their yellow pom-poms, cheering me on. At long last, I had found it, a retort to my father. *We matter, we matter*. In tangible, concrete ways human beings matter to this planet, to society, to one another. It was not a lie to say so. Not a sappy cop-out or a sin. It was Darwin's creed! It was, conversely, a lie to say only that we didn't matter and keep it at that. That was too gloomy. Too rigid. Too shortsighted. Dirtiest word of all: unscientific.

I gave the steering wheel a little tap. My fingers felt lighter on the vinyl, more in command of the life they steered.

But there was still the problem of what I was driving toward, what we all were driving toward, in our cars with our headlights and our hope. That same empty horizon. I was still sure that our ruler was uncaring and cold, that waiting around the corner for each of us was precisely nothing. No promises. No refuge. No gleaming. No matter what we did or how much we mattered to one another.

But that was because I hadn't yet come to understand the final chapter of David's story. An existentially shocking surprise ending waiting in the wings.

13.

Deus ex Machina

I t was a temperate morning in September when David Starr Jordan finally met his end. He was eighty years old. He was at home, surrounded by his menagerie of loved ones, canine, avian, botanical, human. The day before, he had suffered a powerful stroke—his brain's electricity finally betraying him. He passed from this world gently, the eucalyptus trees carrying his last breaths away on their mists of mint and pine, the firethorn bushes offering applause with their brilliant orange berries just coming into bloom. As the earth slowly turned to face the sun, there's a chance that his very last vision was his very first love: the twinkling light of the last stars lingering in the twilight sky.

Shortly after the anniversary of David's death, his wife, Jessie, threw a little garden party in his honor. She opened the gates of their home to the schoolchildren of California. Would anyone come? she wondered. Would anyone care? Would opinion about her dear eugenicist of a husband have already turned? According to the papers, they came by the hundreds. Droves of children, wearing garlands and swinging baskets, and descending on "the great humanitarian's garden . . . as they would a shrine."

And the reverence for David Starr Jordan seemed only to solidify over time. If you stroll Stanford's campus today, you will find a bronze bust of him in the library, a psychology building bearing his name, portraits of him in ornate frames. His biographer, Edward McNall Burns, encapsulates his life this way:

> Few men have lived lives more balanced, harmonious, and fruitful. . . . He turned out to be one of the most versatile men America has produced, winning distinction not only as an educator, philosopher, and scientist but as an explorer, a crusader for peace and democracy, and an adviser to Presidents and foreign statesmen. The breadth of his genius can be measured by the facts that a mountain peak and a biological law were named in his honor, and he was awarded a prize of $25,000 for the best plan of education to promote international peace. It would seem no exaggeration to say that he belonged to the great tradition of the eighteenth century, personified by such giants as Franklin and Jefferson.

Oh, and as for that international peace prize! It turned out David would spend a great deal of his later years, in the run-up to World War I, traveling the globe to warn diplomats against the dangers of war, facing so much resistance he was once stopped mid-speech by a German general who commanded, *"Genug!"* (Enough!) And why? Why was he so committed to the unpopular cause of pacifism? Because, David reasoned, war depleted a nation of its best and brightest. The death of his brother, Rufus, had never left him. The highest-quality men went to fight and die, he explained, leaving the "unfit" to reproduce. "[I]f a nation sends forth the best it breeds to destruction," he said to an audience of hundreds gathered in Philadelphia, "the second best will take their vacant places. The weak, the vicious, the unthrifty will propagate and . . . have the land to themselves." In other words, he was a pacifist as a means of accomplishing his eugenicist ends.

More than four thousand feet above sea level, standing amid the Sierra Nevadas, you will find his mountaintop. Jordan Peak. It is sprinkled with orange and white alpine lilies; it is closer to the sun than many of us will ever get. And it doesn't stop there. All across the country, there are significant entities named in his honor, including two high schools, a government ship, a city boulevard, a stretch of river in Indiana, two lakes (one in Alaska and one in Utah), a prestigious scientific award (which comes with a $20,000 cash prize), and more than a hundred species of fish. *Jordan's snapper. Jordan's grouper. Jordan's sole.*

David estimated that of the 12,000–13,000 species of fish known to humans in his day, he and his students had discovered over 2,500 of them. Meaning, from the time of cavemen to his present day, he and his disciples unveiled nearly a fifth of that scaly section of the tree of life. The fact that many of his fish were in fact discovered by the very targets of his eugenicist campaign—the immigrants and "paupers" whose value to society he dismissed—was something David chose to omit from the scientific record. Recent scholarship by Jessica George shows how heavily David relied on immigrant labor on his 1880 trip up the Pacific coast, at times using intimidation tactics to force Chinese and Chinese-American fishermen to fork over their best catches. David himself admits that often it was a "small boy" or "half-breed" or "Portuguese lad" who led him to, and *caught*, new fish species. He estimates: "Of the hundred or more new species of rock-pool fishes lately secured by the writer in Japan, fully two-thirds were obtained by Japanese boys. Equally effective is the 'muchacho' on the coasts of Mexico." He felt no need to officially credit these people, however, and thus their work, their expertise, their discoveries, went down in the history books as his. He also felt no need to mention how severely his allergy to formaldehyde and ethanol impacted his ability to handle specimens. His colleague George S. Meyers later conjectured that David made "few to none" of the actual measurements of his fish after 1885. No matter. His legacy as the swashbuckling giant of fish discovery remains untarnished. As two contemporary ichthyologists estimate it, the "impact of David Starr Jordan has been so pervasive that it is difficult, if not impossible, to measure. . . . Almost all systematic ichthyologists in North America can trace their scientific or intellectual descent to him."

Sigh.

That's how his story ends. David Starr Jordan was allowed to emerge unscathed, unpunished for his sins, because this is the world in which we live. An uncaring world with no sense of cosmic justice encoded anywhere in its itchy, meaningless fabric.

And yet that is not the end. Because our world, our bottomlessly chaotic world, had one more trick up her sleeve. One last way of wrecking David's order, of stealing away that thing most precious to him.

Did you see it there? Flashing across the spectacles of the taxonomists, refracting off their scalpels, glimmering across the cover of this very book—the insidious way that Chaos finally demolished his fish collection once and for all?

It wasn't lightning or flood or decay or a massive sinkhole opening up and swallowing them all away. No, she had a far crueler method. She made him do it by his very own hand.

What David Starr Jordan set in motion by practicing the art of taxonomy, by following Darwin's advice to sort creatures by evolutionary closeness, led to a fateful discovery. In the 1980s taxonomists realized that fish, as a legitimate category of creature, do not exist.

Birds exist.

Mammals exist.

Amphibians exist.

But fish, in particular, do not exist.

✳   ★   ✳

I first heard about this trippy-sounding idea in Carol Kaesuk Yoon's marvelous book *Naming Nature*. I had set out simply to learn a bit more about the field of taxonomy, and Yoon's was the most recent book on the topic. I hoped to find out a bit about Linnaeus, to learn a little Darwin, a little DNA, so I could better understand the scientific landscape through which David Starr Jordan's story roamed. What I found between those pages astounded me.

Yoon's personal story collides with, as she terms it, "The Death of the Fish." In the 1980s she was in grad school getting a biology degree, happily believing fish were very much in existence, when a new breed of scientists called "cladists" (or "raving cladists," as Yoon says they were often called) strolled through the door. Their name comes from the Greek *klados*, for branch. And it was branches they were after. They were dead set on determining the true branches of the evolutionary tree, human intuition be damned. Their first rule was simple. A legitimate evolutionary group must include *all* descendants of a given ancestor, no extras. You could move as far up or down the tree as you wanted to start a group. You wanna talk vertebrates? Great. That includes all creatures with a backbone. Snakes? In. Worms? Out. You wanna talk mammals? Fine. Must include every single descendant of that first creature able to make milk. Cats, dogs, whales, all good. No reptiles allowed! You get it.

Now, the cladists' other big rule concerned how to answer that most simple-sounding but difficult of questions: Who is most closely related to whom? It might sound trivial, but this is the entire puzzle of taxonomy. In a world of nipples and whiskers and quills, how on earth do you decide which attributes provide the soundest clues? At the time of the cladists' arrival on the scene, there was a technique in vogue called "numerical taxonomy." Its hope was that computers could determine evolutionary closeness by brute force.

You'd simply punch in *as many* characteristics as you could think to compare between species (if it was birds, for example: beak type, egg size, feather color, vertebrae count, intestine length, etc.), and it would spit out likely patterns of relationship. The thinking was that the more similarities two species had, the more closely they were related. But the relationships the computer suggested often made no sense at all. Removing human intuition entirely . . . left you with Chaos.

The cladists, however, realized that certain characteristics were more useful than others. The ones that could reliably show you the passage of time through species were what they called "shared evolutionary *novelties*." The new additions. A brand-new set of antennae, say, or a shiny yellow fin. If you could locate the novel upgrades to the model, you could follow them through different iterations of creatures (or plants) and guess, with more confidence, which way the arrow of time was pointing. You could declare, with greater confidence, who begot whom.

It was simple. It was subtle. It was genius. And, in time, it would reveal some very surprising relationships. Like, for example, as much as a bat might look like a winged rodent, it's actually more closely related to camels. Or that whales are actually ungulates (the family to which deer belong)!

Yoon recalls the cladists striding into her classroom, eager to pin up their racy new drawings of the tree of life. They would point out some of the most stunning examples of what intuition had obscured. The fact that birds are dinosaurs. Or that mushrooms, as plantlike as they *feel*, are actually more closely related to animals. But usually, they'd save the best for last, seeming to take particular delight in what Yoon called "the ritual killing of the fish."

She said that they would begin by pointing to pictures of three animals. A cow. A salmon. A lungfish. *Which of these things was not like the other?* they would ask. Which creature was most *distantly related* from the group? And inevitably some poor, unsuspecting student would raise a hand and pick the cow. *The cow is least like the two fish.*

"At about this point," Yoon explains, "a wicked smile would spread across the cladist's face as he proceeded to show you exactly why you were wrong."

The cladists would remind you to focus on finding the shared evolutionary *novelties.* If you could, for just one moment, not be blinded by the cloak of scales, then you would begin to notice other, more revealing similarities. The lungfish and the cow, for instance—both have lung-like organs that allow them to breathe air, while the salmon does not. The lungfish and the cow both have an epiglottis (a small flap of skin that covers the windpipe). The salmon? Alas, epiglottis-less. And the lungfish's heart is structured more like a cow's than a salmon's. The list goes on and on. Leading the students, finally, to the conclusion that the lungfish is more closely related to the cow than to the salmon.

And that's when they would begin really revving their proverbial chain saws at the tree of life. According to Yoon, the cladists would say that once you accept this—that many of the fishy-looking creatures swimming in the water are more closely related to mammals than to each other—you begin to see a strange truth unfolding before your eyes. That "fish" as a sound evolutionary category is totally bunk. It would be like saying, as Yoon puts it, "all the animals with red spots on them" are in the same category, "or all the mammals that are loud." Fine, it's a category you can make. But it's scientifically meaningless. It tells you nothing about evolutionary relationships.

Still confused? Picture it another way. Imagine that for millennia we silly humans incorrectly believed that all creatures that lived on mountaintops were members of the same evolutionary group, called "mish." The fish of the mountain. Mish. Okay. So mish includes mountain goats, and mountain toads, and mountain eagles, and mountain men—burly and bearded and enjoying their whiskey. Now let's just pretend that, even though all these creatures are incredibly different from one another, they all happened to evolve a similar protective outerwear to survive at that altitude. Let's imagine that outerwear is not scales but plaid. They are all plaid. Plaid eagles. Plaid toads. Plaid men. Such that they *appear*, what with their habitat (mountaintop) and their skin type (plaid), to be the same kind of creature. They are mish. We falsely believed them to be all of a kind.

We have done the same thing with fish—subjugated a world of nuance down into the word "fish."

In reality, down in the water, beneath their costumes of scales exist all kinds of creatures, as varied as those on the mountaintop. There are the Sarcopterygii, quite close to us—the lungfish and coelacanths—our evolutionary cousins in a sense, mermaids with lungs on top, tails down low. Then, across some huge evolutionary divide are the Actinopterygii. Salmon. Bass. Trout. Eels. Gar. Though they appear like twins of the Sarcopterygii—slimy and scaly and fishy as can be—on the inside, they are a world apart. Then you've got the sharks and rays, the Chrondrichthyes, as they are called. A puzzling group. In their smooth skin and voluptuous bodies, I always thought I recognized a closeness to mammals. But it turns out that they are even further from us than the scaly trout and eels. Much older, evolutionarily. Keep skimming down the tree, getting closer and closer to the origin of life, and you'll find the Myxini (don't look them up—as adorable as they sound, they are the sucker-mouthed, razor-toothed stuff of nightmares), which are often grouped together with the snake-like lampreys into a family called Agnatha. After that come the sea squirts (or tunicates), those sessile creatures that David Starr Jordan loved to point to as cautionary tales in laziness. While not technically vertebrates (according to today's taxonomists, anyway), these creatures were some of the first to pioneer a backbone-like structure—a cartilage mast called a notochord. They were innovators, in other words, the very antonym of *backslider*.

The category "fish" hides all of this. Hides nuance. Discounts intelligence. It gerrymanders close cousins away from us, creating a false sense of separation to preserve our spot at the top of an imaginary ladder.

Now, look. If you are still hell-bent on keeping *all* fishy-looking things together as one scientifically valid group, you *can* do that. You can push those scaly lungfishes and coelacanths back into the water with the trout and the goldfish, where you think they belong. And you can even call that category "fish"! It's just that to do that, you'd need to throw a few other creatures into the group so that every single descendant of their shared ancestor was included.

Those frogs perched there on the water's edge? Kick 'em in.

Those birds flying high in the sky? Drown 'em.

Cows, of course, they're in.

Your mom? Absolutely. A fish.

No, the more scientifically logical thing to do is to admit that fish, all this time, have been a delusion. Fish don't exist. The category "fish" doesn't exist. That category of creature so precious to David, the one that he turned to in times of trouble, that he dedicated his life to seeing clearly, was never there at all.

To get a sense of how far the disappearance had spread, I asked the guardians of our national collection of fish at the Smithsonian. I wanted to find out: Did working fish scientists really no longer believe in their object of study? That day I visited to see David Starr Jordan's namesake fish in the locked facility in Maryland, I asked the two taxonomists leading me around, with a little dare in my voice: "Do fish *exist?*" And Dave Smith, who has been working as a taxonomist for half a century, exhaled a few equivocations and conceded, finally, "Probably not." He explained that when the cladists first showed up, he didn't want to believe them. They were too "aggressive," to the point of seeming like fanatics. But in time, he realized that if he was interested in doing his job well, in uncovering the true interconnections of life, he couldn't deny what they were saying: that "fish," really, when you looked straight at it, was a bum category. Slippery, sloppy, what taxonomists call "paraphyletic"— missing some of its members. Later, I called up one of the head curators of the American Museum of Natural History's Ichthyology Department, Melanie Stiassny, to see if the fish had disappeared from her ranks too. "Oh, gosh," she said. "That's broadly accepted." Deadpan, as you can imagine.

"It's counterintuitive!" Rick Winterbottom, a self-confessed "raving cladist," told me. He knows that more than anyone. For more than three decades, he has been trying to convince his students that the natural world does not actually arrange itself into the categories we set for it. And he has been dismayed to watch how little the idea has spread outside academia. He worries that he is up against an opponent far too mighty: intuition. That people will never exchange comfort for truth.*

---

* Welcome to my only footnote in the book! Thanks for joining me here. Your reward is learning about the crazy factoid that there may even be an order of the natural world wired into us. Carol Kaesuk Yoon writes about the incredible medical case of J.B.R., a British patient in the 1980s who accidentally damaged this piece of neurological machinery (Yoon, 12–13) after a case of herpes caused his brain to swell. J.B.R. awoke anew, suddenly unable to properly distinguish between basic categories in the natural world. He couldn't tell the difference between a cat and a carrot, a toadstool and a toad. It was all . . . Chaos. But *oddly*, the nonliving world was completely intact. He understood the difference between a car and a bus, a table and a chair, no problem. It was only the living world that was in shambles. What his case and others (just google

Carol Kaesuk Yoon had a hard time deprogramming herself. She writes:

I found it particularly painful to see [the fish] die, be killed really, as I did, again and again, in lecture halls, in seminar rooms, in laboratories, at scientific meetings, in quiet hallways, as a tender young graduate student. As right as I knew the science behind it was, it always hurt a bit. . . . [F]ollowing along the brutally tidy cladistics logic, I often felt as if I'd somehow been tricked, fooled by some kind of sleight of hand. And I was not alone. You could practically hear people thinking, Hey, wait a minute, how'd you do that? What did you do with the fish . . . ? It was much more than a mere trick. It was the stark naked truth.

Yoon's pain here is precious to me, the "brutal[ity]" of her experience of letting go of the fish. Because I take her as a proxy for David Starr Jordan. Knowing him, his belief that a scalpel would show him the "true relations" between creatures, I *do* believe he would have eventually come to accept the death of the fish. He would have skinned a marbled lungfish, say, and glimpsed its lungs, its epiglottis, its multi-chambered heart, and felt the category dissolving between his fingertips. But knowing how precious fish were to

---

"category-specific semantic deficits" to find them) suggest is that there may be a kind of order-creating mechanism inside of us—that we come into the world predisposed to acquire a very specific set of beliefs about how to sort nature. Who belongs together, who belongs apart, who belongs on top. Other studies have shown how early we seem to obey these intuitive rules: at four months old we begin differentiating between cats and dogs, for example. The fact that this intuitive order may be a part of our wiring does not mean it is truth. It means it is *useful*. It means that it has served our species well over the generations, helped us to so successfully navigate and exploit the Chaos around us.

him—his salve in times of anguish, his sense of purpose—I don't think it would have been easy.

His hurt, imagining him in some degree of anguish . . . it has a wonderful effect. It makes my skin prickle with the most forbidden of atheist fantasies. That somehow, out there, encoded in the cold math of Chaos, there is a sort of cosmic justice after all.

It's right about now that I picture the fisherman.

He is digging his hand down into a bucket of oily trout, and his palm curls around a particularly thick one, and he slaps it—*thud*— right over the words *Fish don't exist.*

And then he sells that trout for money. Because that trout exists. And I know.

I know how he feels.

Besides some sick satisfaction I get from watching the universe steal David Starr Jordan's beloved fish from him, did it matter? Did it matter, in any broader sense, to anyone whose job is not arranging specimens in jars, that fish, as a category, does not exist?

It was a question that was beginning to haunt me. After years of researching these ideas, after covering my little room in Heather's apartment with jagged new drawings of the tree of life, after feeling my heart swell with the thrill that the world beneath our feet was not what we thought it was, I would, in the same breath, get hit with the worry that it was all just semantics. A linguistic party trick. *Fish don't exist.* Big whoop.

So, one night, after Heather got home from work, I decided to talk to her about it. She had become nonconsensually well versed in the topic due to my infatuation with it. I let her take off her coat and get settled on the couch. Then I brought out a plate of cheese and crackers, and asked the thing I feared: "Do you think any of this matters?"

And Heather looked at me, aghast. "Of *course* it matters!" she said.

She brought up, of all people, Copernicus. She spoke about how hard it must have been for people in his day to look up at the stars and fathom that the stars were not the ones moving. But still, it mattered, to talk about it, to think about it, to do the mental scrunching that allowed oneself to slowly let go of the idea of the stars as a celestial ceiling that rotated over one's head each night. Because, as she said: "When you give up the stars you get a universe. So what happens when you give up the fish?"

I had no idea. But I knew in that moment, that was it. That waiting on the other side of the fish was something else. That letting go of the fish would result in some sort of existential exchange.

And I figured the result would be different for everyone.

Just as it had been with the stars.

For some, the letting go of the stars was horrifying. It made them feel too small, too pointless, too out of control. They would not believe it. They shot the messengers. When Copernicus gave up the stars, he was condemned as a heretic. When Giordano Bruno gave up the stars, he was burned at the stake. When Galileo gave up the stars, he was placed under house arrest.

For others, it inspired ambition, invention, engineering. Generations of humans would grow up hell-bent on figuring out how to launch ships to the other side of intuition. Their wildest dreams are why we can now lay hands upon the moon.

For me, when I gave up the stars, as a child on the deck that morning with my dad, I got a breeze—a sense of spinning through the cosmos pointlessly, which on bad days could leave me with a near-fatal chill.

When my father gave up the stars, he got the freedom to invent his own morality, to flout any rules he deemed pointless—return addresses, sleeves, not eating your lab mice.

I'm sure giving up the stars has a different effect on a priest. A nomad. A baker. A candlestick maker.

So, too, with the fish.

When Carol Kaesuk Yoon gave up the fish, she developed a sort of rage at the scientific community she had revered her whole life. A worry that by stealing away human intuition, you leave the general public caring even *less* about the environment—which so desperately needs our affection. Despite a book so beautifully articulating the death of the fish, a part of her yearns for a return to simple language.

When Rick Winterbottom, the aforementioned raving cladist, gave up the fish, he got Purpose. He toured the nation with a cause. He executed fish after fish on chalkboard after chalkboard, eager to pull the wool from people's eyes. He felt that he was rewiring himself, that he was getting a little bit closer to the truth, and he was eager to help others peer through the portal. Now, decades later, he's deflated. By how few people have accepted this new vision. By how little he's been able to chip away at people's certainty. "It's been a constant battle for, uh, thirty years," he sighed, "so now I take it out on a golf ball instead. My new ambition is to carpet the forest floors and lake bottoms with little white spherical objects . . . and I'm doing a pretty good job of it."

When Trenton Merricks, the UVA philosopher who does not believe in chairs, gave up the fish, he got another arrow in his quiver. "I'm not that shocked," he told me after I breathlessly informed him of the dissolution of the category. This is exactly what he's trying to get his students to understand. That we barely know the world around us, even the simplest things under our feet. That we have been wrong before and we will be wrong again. That the true path to progress is paved not with certainty but doubt, with being "open to revision."

When Anna gave up the fish—well, she hasn't really. But she asked if it was sort of like the term "unfit." That word that had been slapped onto her back, and used to throw her behind brick walls, steal her childhood, and cut off her chances of carrying on. I said that, yes, it was very much like that. She nodded. She said she had sympathy for the fish, then. Sympathy for the idea that once you name something, you tend to stop looking at it.

When ethologist Jonathan Balcombe gave up the fish—or, to be fair, he says he'd like to see the genetic studies before he officially cashes in the term, but the idea lines up with what he's observed—he got the feeling of convergence. He had already written a whole book, called *What a Fish Knows: The Inner Lives of Our Underwater Cousins*, that shows how vast and complex their cognitions appear to be. How they see more colors than us, how they can outperform us on certain memory tasks, use tools, differentiate between Bach and the blues. How some species appear to experience pain. I asked Balcombe, jokingly, what everyone was supposed to do, ha, stop eating fish, ha? He quietly said, "Yeah." I'm not there yet, but I do agree with his thesis: that swimming in that water are creatures with far more cognitive complexity than we typically think. That "fish," in a certain sense, is a derogatory term. A word we use to hide that complexity, to keep ourselves comfortable, to feel further away from them than we actually are.

The famous primatologist Frans de Waal, of Emory University, says this is something humans do all the time—downplay similarities between us and other animals, as a way of maintaining our spot at the top of our imaginary ladder. Scientists, de Waal points out, can be some of the worst offenders—employing technical language to distance the other animals from us. They call "kissing" in chimps "mouth-to-mouth contact"; they call "friends" between primates "favorite affiliation partners"; they interpret evidence showing that crows and chimps can make tools as being somehow qualitatively different from the kind of toolmaking said to define humanity. If an animal can beat us at a cognitive task—like how certain bird species can remember the precise locations of thousands of seeds—they write it off as instinct, not intelligence. This and so many more tricks of language are what de Waal has termed "linguistic castration." The way we use our tongues to disempower animals, the way we invent words to maintain our spot at the top.

My dad won't give up the word "fish." He says he likes it too much. He understands that it's scientifically inaccurate, but he finds it useful. When I ask him if he cares that in using it he is imprisoning himself in a limited way of experiencing the world, he groans and says, "Eh. I'm too old to be freed of anything I haven't already been freed from."

My oldest sister had no problem letting go of the fish. She let the whole category slide right out of her hand. When I asked her why it was so easy for her, she said, "Because it's a fact of life. Humans get things wrong." She said people have been wrong about her, time and time again, for her whole life. She's been misdiagnosed by doctors, misunderstood by classmates, by neighbors, by our parents, by me. "Growing up," she told me, "is learning to stop believing people's words about you."

It is different for everyone.

Epilogue

still didn't know what I got when I gave up the fish.

I knew that it was time to leave Chicago. That I couldn't hide out in my purgatory anymore. That as comfortable as it had felt to stay in Heather's apartment, this second-story nest warmed by Heather's belief that the curly-haired man might someday return to me, I had to get on with my life, to step back into the Chaos and see what happened.

I scrambled around until I found myself a temp job, working as a producer on the science desk at National Public Radio. I hoped that work alone could fill my sails. I doubted it could.

One cold February afternoon I drove my little purple car to Washington, DC. I unloaded my belongings into a basement apartment, with a bed in the kitchen and two windows near the ceiling. The trees were barren and the days were short and the world felt bleak.

I walked to work every day. One day I got mugged. One day I turned thirty. I knew almost nobody in the city. I felt like an impostor at NPR. I felt that people could see the truth, that I was a ditz, a klutz, an underqualified journalist, a slut, a cheater, a bad guy.

I had trouble making eye contact. I did a run of stories about people who are blind. There was a calm, in all honesty, in being around people who couldn't see me. I often thought about the curly-haired man. I often thought about a gun.

One day, spring came. I was on a run, sprinting up a hill in a neighborhood I had never run in before. The treetops had come alive with white puffs of petals. I reached the top of the hill. There was a park awaiting, with benches, a small fountain, an intricate garden with daffodils and poofy blue flowers and ferns. I removed my earbuds, began to walk into it. I heard a few birds chirping. Some buzzing something near my face. A dragonfly? A bee? I wasn't sure. I had a sudden vision. Of curtains. Victorian curtains, printed in a nature pattern of the very creatures and plants at which I was looking. Ferns. Dragonflies. Hummingbirds. I had this shimmery sense that all the stuff I was looking at, whose order I had never truly questioned . . .

- the bird, a clear inferior, though admirable for its acrobatic feats;
- the dragonfly, a faraway soul, barely animal (a twig with wings);
- the tree, the mightiest of the plants;
- the mushroom, its deformed little brother

. . . was totally wrong. That this intuitive hierarchy was like the curtains. A man-made design drawn over nature, pleasing to the human eye, perhaps, but arbitrary. I pictured the curtains billowing, revealing the glimpse of a window beyond.

I wanted so badly to see past them, past the lines we draw over nature, to the land that Darwin promised was there, to the land that the taxonomists could see, the gridless place where fish don't exist and nature is more boundless and bountiful than anything we can imagine.

"There is another world, but it is in this one," says a quote attributed to W. B. Yeats that I kept tacked to my wall for years. That was the world I wanted to see. I tried finding it in interviews with scientists, in documentaries about nature, in whiskey. Nothing.

It would take a snorkel.

The plastic pressed hard against my nose, for me to finally see it. Let me explain.

I met a girl. A few months after that run. In July. In a bar. Her face was covered in glitter. She was younger than me. Shorter than me. She was a girl. Many things that did not fit my criteria for a "mate."

If I'd still been stuck on the form of the curly-haired man, I would have missed her.

I kissed her. This was not so strange. Kissing girls, as I knew too well, was something I liked to do. But I had always thought it was for fun, that they tasted good but would be too hard to live with. I was sure I needed a man. To calm my soul and make me feel small and protected against the big bad world.

But, man, did she taste good. Like lavender and rubies and the hard-candy lies you roll around on your tongue to cut class. She made me laugh. One summer night, lying in bed with her, she said out of the blue, "I respect your sexuality," referring to the fact that I should be classified as bisexual. Bisexual. Bi. It was a word I hated. That felt somehow both reductive and accusatory. But I thought it was incredibly sweet of her to honor my multitudes. Then her face crinkled into laughter: "Even if society doesn't!" I tried to swat her shoulder, but she dodged.

I couldn't keep up with her. One day, while riding bikes along the Potomac River, she started racing me, and I couldn't catch her. I ran five miles most days. And I couldn't catch her. I liked that feeling. Her mind was faster than mine, too. She could drum up dazzling rants about tentative drivers, about scrambled eggs, about people who sign their emails with only one initial. "Are you *that* busy?!" she groaned. "Are you that beholden to the cult of overwork that you need to communicate that you do not even have those four milliseconds to spare?" She had a way with words. She called certain dark, off-kilter days "Paul Bowlsey." She once described the way her heart was ripping open with new love for her mother as "ravine-ing." She was great at building fires, could get one going out of wet leaves and a single match. She said she wanted to get so good she could control the way the smoke went.

I told myself I would not worry about what any of it meant until October. October came and went, quickly. One day, plum in the middle of it, we purchased tickets to Bermuda. She was furloughed from her job as a government scientist. I faked a cough and we headed out for a three-day weekend trip.

We had picked out the cheapest Airbnb on the island. A small apartment whose dot on the map was far from all the resorts. It was near the airport, near a beach called Tobacco Bay. We braced our-selves as we landed, picturing cigarette butts bobbing in the water, gasoline smeared all over the waves. After our taxi dropped us off, we shed our bags and galloped toward the water.

This is my pen-fails-me moment.

It was an aqua cove enclosed by towering limestone rock forma-tions. Our own private Atlantis. As we ran toward the water, we noticed a small hut at the far end of the beach. It looked deserted. But as we made our way up to inspect it, we discovered there was a man inside selling drinks. And snorkel gear.

The emerald-eyed girl asked if I wanted to rent snorkels. I said no. I had tried it once, long ago, and all I remembered was the taste of rubber, the feel of a constricted nose.

The next morning I went for a long, slow run along the coast, stopping frequently to gaze at the water, to climb inside abandoned forts. When I finally made it back to Tobacco Bay, it had been al-most two hours. I figured I should go up to the apartment to get her, but the thought of plunging into the water right *then*. While my body was still hot. I couldn't resist.

I felt a little guilty as I swam. Here I was being indulgent, again. But then, before I knew it, she appeared. From—I didn't understand where. Like a mermaid, she popped up from the water, way out toward the horizon. As she got closer, I saw that she was grinning, big and goofy, beneath a snorkel mask.

"Here," she said, unsquelching it from her face. "Try it."

I squeezed the mask over my eyes. Dipped my head below.

I don't know if it was the endorphins.

The clarity of the water.

What.

But the fish.

They were like nothing I had ever seen.

Yellow parrots and black angels and aquamarine slices of the moon. A purplish one, of substantial size, let me chase it around like a puppy. I whooped, but it was too muted. I had to come up above the water to let the whoop register properly. I went back under. There they were. These creatures I had read so much about. Whose names I still did not know. All I knew was that underneath their skin were organs more similar to mine than I used to imagine, brains whirring with the very same ions as mine. All I knew was that they were not fish. A school of silver beings came rushing toward me, barreling beneath me like a catchable train. I dove down into it. It parted and let me in. Hundreds of silver souls enveloping me.

I came up for a gulp of air.

She was still there. I didn't know how long it had been. Five seconds. Three days. We swam out, farther and farther away from the safety of the little beach, rounding the corner of limestone cliffs. The water was choppier out there, darker and cooler, but the fish seemed even brighter, wilder. I'd watch as she would dive down toward the submerged rocks and explosions of neon fish would burst from the cracks and encircle her, swirling over her back, through her armpits, nearly grazing the teal cloth of her bikini. She was a part of them. *We are all fish,* I thought. Maybe. Though probably not. Cold and colors leaving no room for such thoughts. I was thinking. *Snorkel is best invention. God bless snorkel inventor. It win peace prize?*

Then something went wrong. Her swimming went suddenly labored. She was tugging at something near her hip. And we were so far away. And then. She will kill me for typing it. And then. She released the teal triangle of fabric from between her legs and swam out before me, liberated, frog-kicking just to let me look . . . through the clarity of a snorkel . . . to look.

I knew then that I was done.

I NEVER WANT A LIFE WITHOUT THIS PERSON, was the thought.

This was not the life I had envisioned, chasing after a pint-size woman, seven years my junior, who beats me on bikes and rolls her eyes at me a lot. But it is the life I want. I broke through the category. Peered beyond those nature-printed curtains. Saw the world for what it is, a place of infinite possibility. All categories, imaginary. It was the best feeling in the world.

Now when I lie in bed next to my emerald-eyed wife, and the gun comes—and it still comes, will probably always still come—I consider its offerings. The relief it could bring. The solution to that day's stresses and messes I have made. An end to shame.

And then I consider the fish. The fact that fish don't exist. I picture a silvery fish dissolving in my hand. If fish don't exist, what else don't we know about our world? What other truths are waiting behind the lines we draw over nature? What other categories are about to cave in? Could clouds be animate? Who knows. On Neptune, it rains diamonds; it really does. Scientists figured that out just a few years ago. The longer we examine our world, the stranger it proves to be. Perhaps there will be a mother waiting inside a person deemed unfit. Perhaps there will be medicine inside a weed. Salvation inside the kind of person you had discounted.

When I give up the fish, I get, at long last, that thing I had been searching for: a mantra, a trick, a prescription for hope. I get the promise that there are good things in store. Not because I deserve them. Not because I worked for them. But because they are as much a part of Chaos as destruction and loss. Life, the flip side of death. Growth, of rot.

The best way of ensuring that you don't miss them, these gifts, the trick that has helped me squint at the bleakness and see them more clearly, is to admit, with every breath, that you have no idea what you are looking at. To examine each object in the avalanche of Chaos with curiosity, with doubt. Is this storm a bummer? Maybe it's a chance to get the streets to yourself, to be licked by raindrops, to reset. Is this party as boring as I assume it will be? Maybe there will be a friend waiting, with a cigarette in her mouth, by the back door of the dance floor, who will laugh with you for years to come, who will transmute your shame to belonging.

I am not saying I'm always so good at looking at the world in this way. I cling to my certainty—teddy bear that it is—and my grudges stay intact; my fear stays charged, the earth flat. But then I read a news article about, say, a new organ discovered in the human body called the "interstitium." There all along but somehow missed by millennia of humans. And the world cracks open a bit. I am reminded to do as Darwin did: to wonder about the reality waiting

behind our assumptions. Perhaps that unsightly bacteria is producing the oxygen you need to breathe. Perhaps that heartbreak will
prove to be a gift, the hard edge off which you reluctantly bounce
to find a better match. Perhaps even your dreams need examining.
Perhaps even your hope . . . needs some doubt.

When I was a sixteen-year-old, I couldn't have known that my
oldest sister would eventually move out, into an apartment about
eight miles from my parents' house. That she would place stick-
ers of flowers all over its walls, that she would line her bed with
stuffed animals, that she would keep her cereal in the fridge. That
she would slowly befriend some of her neighbors, helping that one
old woman with her groceries, helping that one young couple with
their new baby. That she would get into a horrible car accident,
injuring no one but smashing up two cars, and give up driving on
the spot. That afterward, she would begin walking, walking the city
of Boston, walking its sidewalks and bridges and trains, wearing an
aqua-blue fanny pack, chatting with strangers. That a teacher of
classes for adults with disabilities would notice her, and ask her to
co-lead a walking class. That now she walks for a sort of living, she
walks to live. My friends who live in Boston tell me they see her all
the time, walking, her fanny pack bright, smiling. That seeing her
makes them smile, too.

I could not have known how she and my father would become
close in their own, odd sort of way. Over a shared love of breadsticks,
they will go out to their favorite Italian place, just the two of them.
How every once in a while, I will catch her leaning her head on his
shoulder, for just an instant, and in that instant, all the weight of the
planets will recede. How my father's mother, a feisty one, will suddenly fall very ill. How my oldest sister will, in an act so emblematic
of her—her caring, her conscientiousness, her hyper-punctuality—
write and mail my father a condolence card that arrives, somehow,

one day early. How the next day, a few minutes after his mother dies, he will think of my sister's card and he will laugh. The first rupture of warmth on that bleakest of days.

I could not have pictured the walls of the refuge I will find with the emerald-eyed girl. How our porch will be lined with fireflies and rhododendron bushes that occasionally sprout birds' nests, how our lawn won't have much grass, but it will have a firepit—where neighbors sometimes come to torch their Christmas trees and share their sour cherry moonshine—and, eventually, a tiny baby boy who will claw through the dirt toward a patch of overgrown buttercups that we have failed to mow, and push one, *boing*, the finest, *boing*, most interesting, *boing*, toy in the world.

Scientists have discovered, it's true, that employing positive illusions will help you achieve your goals. But I have slowly come to believe that far better things await outside of the tunnel vision of your goals.

When I give up the fish, I get a skeleton key. A fish-shaped skeleton key that pops the grid of rules off this world and lets you step through to a wilder place. The *other world* within this one. The gridless place out the window where fish don't exist and diamonds rain from the sky and each and every dandelion is reverberating with possibility.

To turn the key all you have to do . . . is stay wary of words. If fish don't exist, what else do we have wrong? Slow dawning for me, a scientist's daughter, but when I give up the fish, I realize that science itself is flawed. Not the beacon toward truth I had always thought it was, but a blunt tool that can wreak a lot of havoc along the way. Consider the word "order" itself. It comes from the Latin *ordinem*, to describe a row of threads sitting neatly in a loom. In time, it was extended as a metaphor to describe the way that *people* sit neatly under the rule of a king, general, or president. It was only applied to nature in the 1700s under the assumption—a human fabrication, a superimposition, a guess—that there is an orderly set of ranks to find there. I have come to believe that it is our life's work to tear down this order, to keep tugging at it, trying to unravel it, to set free the organisms trapped underneath. That it is our life's work to mistrust our measures. Especially those about moral and mental standing. To remember that behind every ruler there is a Ruler. To remember that a category is at best a proxy; at worst, a shackle.

Shortly after I first type these words, white supremacists will descend on the town where we live, Charlottesville, Virginia. They will park in front of our house, their wheels kissing the gravel of our driveway. They will storm the park with their swastika shields and their fashionable haircuts to defend a statue of a Confederate leader. They will plow a car over a crowd of protesters, killing one and injuring dozens, and beat a black man bloody with their boots and their boards and their beliefs. After it's all over, their leader will take to the radio. He will express regret for the loss of life, but not the idea. The idea that certain races are higher than others, that white is better than black. It is "just as a matter of science," he will chuckle. A shrug in his tone.

This ladder, it is still alive. This ladder, it is a dangerous fiction. *Fish don't exist.* A fish-shaped sledgehammer to split it down.

My wife stirs next to me in bed. She slaps my shoulder. "Pipe down, Flipper," she mumbles. Referring to the fact that I am flipping, that I am tossing and turning, unable to sleep. She wants me only to join her in peace, in slumber, in the soft cotton waves of our powder-blue sheets. I clutch the brimming warmth of her thigh and think about the fact that even at its most hopeful, my measly brain could have never dreamt up something as infinitely intoxicating as her.

A Note on the Illustrations

The illustrations in this book were made using a direct engraving technique called scratchboard, which originated in the nineteenth century. A white clay hardboard is coated with black India ink and any abrasive can be used to scratch away the black. In this case, the artist primarily used a sewing needle.

Acknowledgments

First and foremost, this book owes its life to its intellectual god-mother, Carol Kaesuk Yoon. If you are even *mildly* interested in the scientific topics discussed within these pages, run, don't walk, to her book *Naming Nature*, which explores in stunning detail the clash of intuition and truth. I am lucky that Yoon was so willing to discuss ideas with me as I was first falling down the rabbit hole of cladistics; she has been a most generous and gracious guide.

Next up, to Heather Radke, who was there from the book's inception. Who made me believe, on a warm couch in a cold city, that any of this was interesting. It's the best gift you can give to a person. Especially a very lonely person. Thank you.

To Aja, Lili, Sarita, Lama, Loi, KK, and Kidda. Whether or not you know it, you have been silent angels in my mind, indestructible sources of support, humor, and encouragement. Thank you for residing there.

To my mother, Robin Feuer Miller, who first taught me to pay attention to The Smalls and whose love was *the* tether through the darkest days.

To Jonathan Fucking Cox! For seeing a light in this book through its barnacles and goiters. And for fighting so hard, against me, to let that light shine. A huge thank-you to Megan Hogan for carrying these pages over home plate, and to Emily Simonson, Janet Byrne, Sara Kitchen, Kirstin Berndt, Julia Prosser, Elise

Ringo, Carly Loman, Alison Forner, and Allison Har-zvi at Simon & Schuster for your hard work and creativity. Thank you also to Jonathan Karp and Richard Rhorer for their willigness to place bad bets. A fact-checked thank-you to fact-checkers Emily Krieger and Michelle Harris. Confirmed, still grateful.

To the best agent there is, Jin Auh, for not only rolling with my crazy but going to bat so hard for it, too.

To all the scholars and thinkers who gave their time to my endless questions, in particular: Paul Lombardo; Dave Catania; Seema Yasmin, Bill Eschmeyer; Chioke I'Anson; Meika Polanco; Rick Winterbottom; Alex Minna Stern; Alison Bell; Daniel Robb; Trenton Merricks; Abby and Guion Pratt; Steve Patterson; Bliss Carnochan; Luther Spoehr; Jonathan Balcombe; Kris Murphy and David G. Smith at the Smithsonian; Coco Wellington, Eileen Casella Rider, and Dorianne Mebane at Penikese Island; Maggie Cutler; Mark Bold; Stanzi Vaubel; Christoph Irmscher; Dina Kellams; Andrea Barbour; the archivists at Stanford University Special Collections, the Hoover Institution, and Indiana University Archives—your tireless help was so appreciated. To Richard White at Stanford and his excellent student scholars, who were generous to share the documents and insights they turned up. Tremendous thanks to Anna and Mary for entrusting me with their stories, and for their time, kindness, and humbling wisdom.

Thank you to the readers who braved early drafts of this thing: Jenny Canton, Alexis Schaitkin, Nell Boesechenstein, Grace Maloney Miller, Heather Radke, Kelley Libby, Robin Feuer Miller, and Chris Miller. The care and time of your notes is a gift that I can probably never repay, but I will sure try. Thank you also to the curly-haired man for letting me share this part of our story and for being not a castle after all, but the best damn greenhouse.

Thank you to my sisters, Abigail and Alexa, for keeping me

honest, for keeping me laughing, and for each teaching me more about how to be strong than anyone on this planet.

Two books to recommend: Daniel Robb's crystalline memoir about his time teaching at the reform school on Penikese Island, *Crossing the Water.* Like the island, the writing is sparse, breathtaking, at times tender, and hard. His questions about the value of seclusion, hard work, and whether a place can change a soul have stayed with me. Secondly, Jennifer Michael Hecht's *Stay: A History of Suicide and the Philosophies Against It*, which lays out a glorious array of nonreligious arguments against killing yourself. Both books are particularly beautiful reads, and gifts I will always cherish.

I am lucky, too lucky, to have been able to train with some of the finest storytellers in our country. Jad Abumrad, Alix Spiegel, Hanna Rosin, Ellen Horne, Kidda Johnson, Anne Gudenkauf, Chenjerai Kumanika, Robert Krulwich, Dominic Preziosi, Chris Tilghman, Chris Pasterczyk, Julia Bator, Pat Walters, and Soren Wheeler: thank you for the time you have each poured into me. It has changed the course of my life. Thank you also to Virginia Humanities, the Virginia Center for the Creative Arts, the University of Virginia's MFA program, and the Awesome Fund, each of which supported this book with the generous gift of funding or space. And to the entire Maloney clan for welcoming me with so much warmth and so much laughter. Your love is even cozier than Nora's favorite couch.

To illustrator Kate Samworth! Seeing you spin images from my words has been the greatest pleasure of this whole experience. For anyone actually reading these acknowledgments, if you are in need of an illustrator, Kate can do it all: oil paint, watercolor, woodcut, scratchboard, even claymation. She is a genius freak of bottomless creativity and wonder. Thank you for lending your immense talent to this project.

Thank you to my dad, Chris Miller, for letting me write so unsparingly about some of your worst moments, for not really caring, for caring so deeply. One finger. By the nose. Forever.

To the Wilcox family, for entertaining my wife and dog when this book kept me away from them. To Bob and Iney, for their bones, and Jeff Werner, for his pyrotechnics.

To sweet Jude, just eleven months old, completely toothless but already smiling at lightning.

And above all, below all, to Grace. Thank you for supporting this book in countless ways; thank you for spilling, and never learning not to burn your tongue. Spending time with you is the grandeur of my life.

Notes

Prologue

4 *a full fifth of fish known to man in his day*: David Starr Jordan, *The Days of a Man: Being Memories of a Naturalist, Teacher and Minor Prophet of Democracy, Volume One, 1851–1899* (Yonkers-on-Hudson, NY: World Book Company, 1922), 288.

Chapter 1: A Boy with His Head in the Stars

9 *"While husking corn"*: Jordan, *The Days of a Man, Volume One*, 21.

9 *he chose "Starr" as his middle name*: Ibid., 21. Jordan says the choice was also partly to honor his "mother's great admiration for the writings of King," ibid.

9 *David's specialty—sewing rags into rugs*: Ibid., 14.

10 *held Rufus in "absolute worship"*: Ibid., 9.

10 *began drawing intricate maps*: Ibid., 3, 11–12, 22, 26.

10 *"The eagerness I then displayed"*: Ibid., 22.

10 *martyr-y accomplishments like never laughing out loud*: Ibid., 3, 4, 7.

10 *potatoes to hoe*: Ibid., 41–44.

10 *Linnaeus's chart was riddled with mistakes*: Louis Agassiz, *Methods of Study in Natural History* (Boston: J. R. Osgood and Company, 1875), 7; Kathryn Schulz, "Fantastic Beasts and How to Rank Them," *The New Yorker*, Oct. 30, 2017.

11 *boats raced more frequently*: Carol Kaesuk Yoon, *Naming Nature: The Clash Between Instinct and Science* (New York: W. W. Norton & Company, 2009), 34–35.

11 *find something "more relevant"*: Jordan, *The Days of a Man, Volume One*, 22.

11 *"The country round about my home"*: Ibid., 24.

11 *"a little book on flowers"*: Ibid.

12 *"I perhaps strained a point"*: Ibid.

12 *"shiftless and a waster of time"*: Ibid.

12 *"The little ones"*: Ibid., 25.

12 *"girls did not consider [him] too promising"*: Edward McNall Burns, *David Starr Jordan: Prophet of Freedom* (Stanford, CA: Stanford University Press, 1953), 2.

13 *tussle with a boy*: Jordan, *The Days of a Man, Volume One*, 17.

13 *quit by his music teacher*: Ibid., 28.

13 *"led off with a broken nose"*: Ibid., 38.

13 *set it on fire*: Ibid., 40.

13 *"clasp [my] hands and jump through them"*: Ibid., 3.

13 *"engaged in the congenial task"*: Ibid., 9.

14 *"I still remember the long period of loneliness"*: Ibid.

14 *explode with color*: Ibid., 27.

14 *The drawings are not artful*: Pencil-and-ink drawings, SC0058, Series II-B, Box 6B, Special Collections and University Archives, Stanford University.

14 *"honey on my lips"*: Jordan, *The Days of a Man, Volume One*, 512.

14 *"deprivation or loss or vulnerability"*: Werner Muensterberger, *Collecting: An Unruly Passion* (Princeton, NJ: Princeton University Press, 1994), 3, 254.

15 *"people have this feeling of personal inefficiency"*: "Collecting Can Become Obsession, Addiction," United Press International, March 15, 2011, https://www.upi.com /Health_News/2011/03/16/Collecting-can-become-obsession-addiction/593013002 99887/?ur3=1.

15 *"exhilarating" to "ruinous"*: Muensterberger, *Collecting: An Unruly Passion*, 6.

15 *"at school no attention"*: Jordan, *The Days of a Man, Volume One*, 24.

15 *trouble finding work*: Ibid., 149–54.

Chapter 2: A Prophet on an Island

19 *with barely any tree cover*: David Starr Jordan, "The Flora of Penikese Island," *The American Naturalist*, Apr. 1874, 193.

19 *the "runt" of its island chain*: Daniel Robb, *Crossing the Water: Eighteen Months on an Island Working with Troubled Boys—a Teacher's Memoir* (New York: Simon & Schuster, 2002), 36.

19 *a "sad and lonely little rock"*: Marlene Pardo Pellicer, "The Outcasts of Penikese Island," *Miami Ghost Chronicles*, Aug. 31, 2018.

19 *an "outpost of hell"*: Elizabeth Mehren, "Disciplinary School for Boys Teaches Some Tough Lessons," *Chicago Tribune*, Aug. 17, 2001.

19 *a leper colony led by a doctor . . . cure his wards*: I. Thomas Buckley, *Penikese: Island of Hope* (Brewster, MA: Stony Brook Publishing, 1997), 72.

19 *"turn a lot of potential murderers into car thieves"*: Dave Masch, as quoted in Daniel Robb, *Crossing the Water: Eighteen Months on an Island Working with Troubled Boys—a Teacher's Memoir* (New York: Simon & Schuster, 2002), 34.

20 *"Study nature, not books"*: Jordan, *The Days of a Man, Volume One*, 118.

20 *locking his students in a closet with dead animals*: Samuel H. Scudder, "In the Laboratory with Agassiz," *Every Saturday*, April 4, 1974, 369–70.

20 *"all the truths which the objects contained"*: William James, *Louis Agassiz: Words Spoken by Professor William James at the Reception of the American Society of Naturalists by the President and Fellows of Harvard College* (Cambridge, MA: Printed for the University, 1897), 9.

20 *"science, generally, hates beliefs"*: Frank Haak Lattin, *Penikese: A Reminiscence by One of Its Pupils* (Albion, NY: Frank H. Lattin, 1895), 54.

21 *"waste chemicals."*: Jordan, *The Days of a Man, Volume One*, 104–6.

21 *"Course of Instruction in Natural History to Be Delivered by the Seaside"*: Lattin, *Penikese: A Reminiscence*, 42.

22 *on July 8, 1873*: Burt G. Wilder, "Agassiz at Penikese," *The American Naturalist*, March 1898, 190.

22 *"botanist in self-defense"*: Jordan, *The Days of a Man, Volume One*, 10.

22 *a lingering shyness in those years, a wariness of new places*: Ibid., 18.

23 *"None of us will ever forget his first sight of Agassiz"*: David Starr Jordan, "Agassiz at Penikese," *Popular Science Monthly*, Apr. 1892, 723.

23 *nor had the shingles*: Wilder, "Agassiz at Penikese," 190–91.

23 *a flimsy sailcloth*: Lattin, *Penikese: A Reminiscence*, 24.

23 *"Viewed simply in itself"*: Ibid., 21.

24 *"'Is this hornblende?'"*: Jordan, *The Days of a Man, Volume One*, 109.

24 *sheep had been dragged out*: Wilder, "Agassiz at Penikese," 191.

24 *Spiderwebs and swallow nests still presided*: Ibid.

24 *Susan Bowen . . . bioluminescence*: "Rest in Peace: Burial of Mrs. Susan B. Jordan," unknown publication, Nov. 17, 1885, David Starr Jordan papers, 000240, Box 38 (Susan Bowen Correspondence), Folder 38-24, Hoover Institution Archives.

24 *"What Agassiz said that morning can never be said again"*: David Starr Jordan, "Agassiz at Penikese," 725.

24 *"The Prayer of Agassiz"*: John G. Whittier and T. W. Parsons, *"The Prayer of Agassiz": A Poem and "Agassiz": A Sonnet* (Cambridge, MA: Riverside Press, 1874), 3–4.

25 *"the thoughts of the Creator"*: Louis Agassiz, *Essay on Classification* (Cambridge, MA: Belknap Press of Harvard University, 1962), 9.

25 *Aristotle first proposed a holy ladder*: Markus Eronen and Daniel Stephen Brooks, "Levels of Organization in Biology," *Stanford Encyclopedia of Philosophy*, Feb. 5, 2018. https://plato.stanford.edu/entries/levels-org-biology/.

26 *"looking heavenward"*: Agassiz, *Methods of Study in Natural History*, 71.

26 *the parrot, the ostrich, and the songbird*: Louis Agassiz, *The Structure of Animal Life: Six Lectures Delivered at the Brooklyn Academy of Music in January and February* (New York: Scribner, 1886), 35.

26 *"the complication or simplicity"*: Agassiz, *Essay on Classification*, 159.

26 *"bestow greater care upon their offspring"*: Agassiz, *Methods of Study in Natural History*, 70.

26 *"true relations"*: Ibid., 7.

26 *"We cannot understand the possible degradation"*: Ibid., 71.

27 *a concept he called "degeneration"*: Louis Agassiz, "Evolution and Permanence of Type," *Atlantic Monthly*, Jan. 1874.

27 *what he called the divine plan*: Agassiz, *Essay on Classification*, 10; Agassiz, *Structure of Animal Life*, 111.

27 *"The swallows flew"*: Jordan, "Agassiz at Penikese," 725.

27 *"A laboratory is a sanctuary where nothing profane should enter"*: Jordan, *The Days of a Man, Volume One*, 118.

27 *"solemn hush"*: Whittier, *"The Prayer of Agassiz,"* 4.

28 *"missionary work of the highest order"*: Jordan, *The Days of a Man, Volume One*, 111.

28 *The rustling of women's bodies*: Ibid., 111–12.

28 *"Agassiz was distinctly stern"*: Ibid., 112.

29 *"Here I made my first acquaintance with fishes"*: Ibid., 119.

Chapter 3: A Godless Interlude

35 *"speck on a speck on a speck"*: Neil deGrasse Tyson, "Space," *Radiolab*, Oct. 21, 2007.

36 *Camus estimates it's on the mind of a majority of us*: Albert Camus, *The Myth of Sisyphus and Other Essays* (New York: Vintage International, 1955), 7.

36 *"grand temptation"*: William Cowper, as cited in Dale Peterson, ed., *A Mad People's History of Madness* (Pittsburgh: University of Pittsburgh Press, 1982), 65.

42 *a small prep school in Appleton*: Jordan, *The Days of a Man, Volume One*, 120.

42 *"one primordial form"*: Charles Darwin, *On the Origin of Species by Means of Natural Selection, or the Preservation of Favoured Races in the Struggle for Life* (Mineola, NY: Dover Publications, 2006), 303.

42 *"species when intercrossed"*: Ibid., 301.

42 *"convenience"*: Ibid., 304.

42 "Natura non facit saltum": Ibid., 288.

43 *evolved from apes "repulsive"*: Agassiz, Methods of Study in Natural History, iv.

43 *"I went over to the evolutionists"*: Jordan, *The Days of a Man, Volume One*, 114.

Chapter 4: Chasing Tail

47 *"literature of Ichthyology"*: Jordan, *The Days of a Man, Volume One*, 140–41.

47 *he set himself the goal*: Ibid., 141.

47 *a flophouse in Indianapolis*: Ibid., 140.

48 *"had appeared as a new species twenty-eight times"*: Ibid., 144.

48 *In 1880, he was sent (as part of the US Census)*: Ibid., 202.

48 *"bright boy"*: "David Starr Jordan Lauds Work of Late C. H. Gilbert," *Indianapolis Star*, July 15, 1928.

48 *"oily" "treasures"* . . . *"which had risen from the deeps in a storm"*: Jordan, *The Days of a Man, Volume One*, 205–9.

48 *"the Spanish flag"*: Ibid., 208.

48 *"the most delicious of all fishes"*: Ibid., 228.

49 *"second-rate shade tree"*: Ibid., 129.

49 *"pirate" with "bad habits"*: Ibid., 212.

49 *make a species degenerate, devolve, or "change for the worse"*: David Starr Jordan, Edwin Grant Conklin, Frank Mace McFarland, and James Perrin Smith, *Foot-Notes to Evo-*

lution: A Series of Popular Addresses on the Evolution of Life (New York: D. Appleton, 1898), 277.

49   *sea squirt . . . "degraded" . . . "idleness," "inactivity and dependence"*: Ibid., 278.

49   *Chinese fishermen*: Ibid., 204, 210, 215, 221.

49   *Portuguese fishermen*: Ibid., 211–12.

49   eighty *new species of fish*: Ibid., 226.

50   *the board of trustees asked him*: Ibid., 288–89.

50   *the youngest university president in the entire country*: Ibid., 297.

51   *"flames of an hour had near undone his life work"*: "Collected from the Ashes!," *Bloomington Telephone*, July 21, 1883.

52   *"To publish at once"*: Jordan, *The Days of a Man, Volume One*, 279.

52   *"rural town doctors were unable to cure"*: Edith Jordan Gardner, "The Days of Edith Jordan Gardner" (unpublished, 1961), SC0058 Series VIII-B, Box 1, Folder 3, Special Collections and University Archives, Stanford University.

52   *"water shone as bright as stars"*: "Rest in Peace: Burial of Mrs. Susan B. Jordan," David Starr Jordan papers, Hoover Institution Archives.

52   *Susan had bemoaned David's traveling*: Multiple correspondences, 1884, David Starr Jordan papers, 000240, Box 38, Hoover Institution Archives (David Starr Jordan to Susan Bowen Jordan, Oct. 24, 1884; Susan Bowen Jordan to her father, Jan. 22, 1884).

52   *"black as the obsidian stone"*: Jordan, *The Days of a Man, Volume One*, 530–33.

53   *"I knew then that I would never call her mother"*: Gardner, "The Days of Edith Jordan Gardner."

53   *"I may only hint"*: Jordan, *The Days of a Man, Volume One*, 326.

53   *"shield of optimism"*: Ibid., 46.

53   *six foot two*: Theresa Johnston, "Meet President Jordan," *Stanford Magazine*, Jan. 2010.

53   *"humming a tune adown the arcade"*: Orrin Leslie Elliott, "David Starr Jordan: An Appreciation," *Stanford Illustrated Review*, Oct. 1931.

53   *"I never worry over a mischance, once it is past"*: Jordan, *The Days of a Man, Volume One*, 46.

54   *the ocean was piped*: Daniel G. Kohrs, "Hopkins Seaside Laboratory of Natural History," *Seaside: History of Marine Science in Southern Monterey Bay*, 2013, 40, https://web.stanford.edu/group/seaside/pdf/hsl4.pdf.

54   *"brilliant" taxonomist*: unnamed reporter, "David Starr Jordan Lauds Work of Late C. H. Gilbert," 1928.

55   *"unfit" . . . "childlike" . . . "sensuous" . . . "playful"*: Louis Agassiz to S. G. Howe, Aug. 10, 1863, as cited in Steven Jay Gould, *The Mismeasure of Man* (New York: W. W. Norton & Company, 1996), 80.

55   *"taught us to think for ourselves"*: Jordan, *The Days of a Man, Volume One*, 113–14.

56   *Escondite, Spanish for "hiding place"*: Ibid., 377.

56   *personal Garden of Eden*: Ibid., 512–13.

56   *"a crowded, incongruous, but delightful jungle"*: Ibid., 512.

56   *"black-eyed Puritan"*: Ibid., 531.

56   *classified it as a waxwing*: Ibid., 23–24.

57   *"the sweetest, wisest, comeliest, and most lovable"*: Ibid., 380.

57   *Unhindered by financial constraints*: Ibid., 289–95.

57   *"flying fox"*: David Starr Jordan, *The Days of a Man: Being Memories of a Naturalist, Teacher and Minor Prophet of Democracy, Volume Two, 1900–1921* (Yonkers-on-Hudson, NY: World Book Company, 1922), 105.

57   *Charley Gilbert getting struck by a falling boulder*: Jordan, *Days of a Man: Volume One*, 263–67.

57   *"fright"*: Ibid., 263.

58   *Jane was not such a fan*: Jane Lathrop Stanford to Horace Davis, Jan. 28, 1905, Special Collections and University Archives, Stanford University, SC0033B, Series I, Box 2, Folder 10, 1–8, https://purl.stanford.edu/sn623dy4566; J. Stanford to David Starr Jordan, Aug. 9, 1904, Ibid.

58   *scientific study of spiritualism*: Robert W. P. Cutler, MD, *The Mysterious Death of Jane Stanford* (Stanford, CA: Stanford University Press, 2003), 32.

58   *David found the notion absurd*: David Starr Jordan to Jane Stanford, Sep. 5, 1904. Special Collections and University Archives, Stanford University, SC0033B, Series I, Box 6, Folder 35, 22–23, https://purl.stanford.edu/hm923kc8513; See also, *Sciosophy* writings.

58   *figure out how the "frauds" worked*: Jordan, *The Days of a Man, Volume One*, 219–20.

58   *"sleight-of-hand performances"*: Ibid., 220.

58   *began publishing*: David Starr Jordan, "The Sympsychograph: A Study in Impressionist Physics," *Popular Science Monthly*, Sept. 18, 1896; David Starr Jordan, "The Principles of Sciosophy," *Science*, May 18, 1900.

58   *"Instruments of precision, logic, mathematics"*: David Starr Jordan, "Science and Sciosophy," *Science*, June 27, 1924, 565.

59   *"trying to believe"*: Ibid., 569.

59   *a "vast amount of suffering in our society"*: David Starr Jordan, "The Moral of the Sympsychograph," *Popular Science Monthly*, Oct. 1896, 265.

59   *accused him of nepotism*: Jane Stanford to Horace Davis, July 14, 1904 (Stanford University Archives), as cited in Cutler, *The Mysterious Death of Jane Stanford*, 107.

59   *"pets"*: Cutler, *The Mysterious Death of Jane Stanford*, 32.

Chapter 5: Genesis in a Jar

63   *certain things don't exist until they get a name*: Author interview, Steve Patterson, Jan. 13, 2017; Author interview, Chioke I'Anson, Dec. 12, 2017; Author interview, Trenton Merricks, Oct. 27, 2017.

63   *Trenton Merricks*: Author interview, Oct. 27, 2017.

68   *Herbert toppled overboard and froze to death*: Jordan, *The Days of a Man, Volume One*, 145.

68   *Charles McKay, went missing*: Ibid., 121.

68   *Charles H. Bollman, who contracted malaria*: Ibid., 238.

68   *hammering them out of coral*: Ibid., 113–14.

68   *"myriads of little fishes"*: David Starr Jordan, *A Guide to the Study of Fishes* (New York: Henry Holt and Company, 1905), 430.

69   *"Walking once with her in the garden"*: Jordan, *The Days of a Man, Volume Two*, 84.

69   *he was too late*: Charles Reynolds Brown, *They Were Giants* (New York: Macmillan, 1934), 202.

69   *"the most cruel personal calamity"*: Jordan, *The Days of a Man, Volume Two*, 83.

70   *she appointed a spy*: Bliss Carnochan, "The Case of Julius Goebel: Stanford, 1905," *The American Scholar*, Jan. 2003, 97; Cutler, *The Mysterious Death of Jane Stanford*, 73.

70   *bearded, bald-headed professor*: Luther William Spoehr, "Freedom to Do Right: David Starr Jordan and the Goebel and Rolfe Cases" (adapted from Luther William Spoehr: "Progress' Pilgrim: David Starr Jordan and the Circle of Reform, 1891–1931," PhD dissertation, Stanford University, 1975), 2.

70   *"incarceration in the insane asylum for sexual perversity"*: Carnochan, "The Case of Julius Goebel: Stanford, 1905," 99.

70   *"whitewashing" a sex scandal*: Goebel to Stanford, June 6, 1904 (Stanford Archives, Horace Davis Papers SC0028, Box 1, Folder 10), as cited in Carnochan, "The Case of Julius Goebel: Stanford, 1905," 99.

70   *"painfully evident to me for a long time"*: Stanford to Davis, July 14, 1904, Stanford University Archives, as cited in Cutler, *The Mysterious Death of Jane Stanford*, 107.

71   *"rumors abounded that Mrs. Stanford planned to replace Jordan"*: Spoehr, "Progress' Pilgrim," 138.

71   *Jane died unexpectedly*: "MRS. STANFORD DIES, POISONED," *San Francisco Evening Bulletin*, March 1, 1905.

71   *David fired the spy from Stanford*: Carnochan, "The Case of Julius Goebel: Stanford, 1905," 101.

71   *he planned another extended tour of Europe*: Jordan, *The Days of a Man, Volume Two*, 158–64.

Chapter 6: Smash

75   *"as if nothing had happened!"*: Jordan, *The Days of a Man, Volume Two*, 168.

75   *7.9 on the Richter scale*: United States Geological Survey, "M 7.9 April 18, 1906 San Francisco Earthquake," https://earthquake.usgs.gov/earthquakes/events/1906calif/.

75   *In just forty-seven seconds*: Abraham Hoffman, *California's Deadliest Earthquakes: A History* (Charleston, SC: History Press, 2017), 2.

75   *over three thousand people were killed*: The National Archives, "San Francisco Earthquake, 1906," https://www.archives.gov/legislative/features/sf.

75   *"as a rat might be shaken by a dog"*: Jordan, *The Days of a Man, Volume Two*, 168.

75   *piano being played by the ceiling falling*: Ibid., 169.

75 *"jumped about in the most violent fashion"*: Ibid., 168.

75 *"had already resumed their singing"*: Ibid., 169.

76 *"gone bum"*: Ibid.

76 *"fall of the beautiful Church tower"*: Ibid.

76 *fallen buttresses*: Molly Vorwerck, "All Shook Up: Stanford's Earthquake History," *Stanford Daily*, Oct. 11, 2013.

76 *"Full of apprehension"*: Jordan, *The Days of a Man, Volume Two*, 169.

78 *headfirst into the concrete*: Photo credit: US Geological Survey, Denver Library Photographic Collection/Walter Curran Mendenhall Collection, 1906.

79 *"the services of a carpenter"*: Jordan to Lathrop, May 24, 1906, Special Collections and University Archives, Stanford University, SC0058, Series II-A, Box 1B-29, Folder 107.

79 *"alcohol [to preserve the fish specimens]"*: Jordan to Greene, May 16, 1906, Special Collections and University Archives, Stanford University, SC0058, Series II-A, Box 1B-29, Folder 107.

79 *"steel wall and floor brace[s]"*: Ettler to Jordan, May 21, 1906, Special Collections and University Archives, Stanford University, SC0058, Series II-A, Box 1B-29, Folder 107.

79 *The alcohol failed to arrive*: Jordan to Greene, May 16, 1906, Special Collections and University Archives, Stanford University.

79 *"The wreckage lay on the floor"*: J. Böhlke, *A Catalogue of the Type Specimens of Recent Fishes in the Natural History Museum of Stanford University (Stanford Ichthyological Bulletin*, Volume 5), ed. Margaret H. Storey and George S. Myers (Stanford, CA: Stanford University, 1953), 3.

79 *He allowed the students to sleep outside on the lawn*: Jordan, *The Days of a Man, Volume Two*, 175.

80 *A thousand times. A thousand fishes gone*: Böhlke, *A Catalogue of the Type Specimens of Recent Fishes*, 3.

81 *this was one of the holotypes*: California Academy of Sciences Ichthyology Collection Database, CatNum: CAS-SU 6509, http://researcharchive.calacademy.org/research/Ichthyology/collection/index.asp?xAction=getrec&close=true&LotID=106509.

81 *through the flesh at the goby's throat*: Ibid., Primary Type Image Base, http://research archive.calacademy.org/research/ichthyology/Types/index.asp?xAction=Search&Rec Style=Full&TypeID=573.

Chapter 7: The Indestructible

87 *"The Eagle and the Blue-Tailed Skink"*: David Starr Jordan, *The Book of Knight and Barbara, Being a Series of Stories Told to Children: Corrected and Illustrated by the Children* (New York: D. Appleton and Company, 1899), 138–40.

88 *In another story, a girl named Barbara is attacked by a coyote*: Ibid., 4–5.

88 *"trying to believe what we know is not true"*: Jordan, "Science and Sciosophy," 569.

88   *Suffering, sickness, ignorance, and war*: Jordan, "The Moral of the Sympsychograph," 265.

88   *Giordano Bruno . . . burned at the stake*: Alberto A. Martínez, "Was Giordano Bruno Burned at the Stake for Believing in Exoplanets?" *Scientific American*, March 19, 2018, https://blogs.scientificamerican.com/observations/was-giordano-bruno-burned-at -the-stake-for-believing-in-exoplanets/.

88   *"Ignorance is the most delightful science in the world"*: Jordan, "Science and Sciosophy," 563.

88   *"Nature no respecter of persons"*: David Starr Jordan, *Evolution: Syllabus of Lectures* (Alameda, CA, 1892), 6–7, SC0058 Series II-B Half Box 7, Special Collections and University Archives, Stanford University.

89   *"forc[e] the nervous system to lie"*: Jordan, *The Days of a Man, Volume One*, 48.

89   *"The fires we kindle die away in coals"*: David Starr Jordan, *The Philosophy of Despair* (San Francisco: Stanley Taylor Company, 1902), 17.

89   *"soul-ache"*: Jordan, Ibid., 14.

89   *"flow of good health"*: Ibid., 30.

89   *"Happiness comes from doing"*: Jordan, *Evolution: Syllabus of Lectures*, 14.

89   *"luscious" taste of a peach*: Jordan, *The Days of a Man, Volume One*, 16.

90   *"lavish" colors of tropical fish*: Jordan, *The Days of a Man, Volume Two*, 115.

90   *"the stern joy which warriors feel"*: Jordan, *Evolution: Syllabus of Lectures*, 14.

90   *"There is no hope for you"*: Jordan, *The Philosophy of Despair*, 33–34.

90   *"fad of the drooping spirit"*: Ibid., 14.

90   *"sad kings'"* . . . *"sulphurous"*: Ibid., 19.

90   *"die while the body is still alive"*: Ibid., 32.

91   *"Do these views of life lead to Pessimism?"*: Jordan, *Evolution: Syllabus of Lectures*, 14.

93   *"Never since man began to plan"*: Jordan, *The Days of a Man, Volume Two*, 177–78.

Chapter 8: On Delusion

98   *Self-delusion was seen as a mental defect*: Shelley E. Taylor and Jonathon D. Brown, "Illusion and Well-Being: A Social Psychological Perspective on Mental Health," *Psychological Bulletin* 103, no. 2 (1988): 193.

98   *"hallmark of mental health"*: Ibid.

98   *mentally healthy people rated themselves as more attractive*: Ibid., 195–97.

98   *They struggled in their lives*: Ibid., 199; Michael Dufner, "Self-Enhancement and Psychological Adjustment: A Meta-Analytic Review," *Personality and Social Psychology Review* 23, no. 2 (2019): 48–72.

99   *good for the bones*: Ibid.

99   *a sense of peace*: Tim Wilson, *Redirect: Changing the Stories We Live By* (New York: Little, Brown and Company, 2011); Gregory M. Walton and Geoffrey L. Cohen, "A Brief Social-Belonging Intervention Improves Academic and Health Outcomes of Minority Students," *Science*, March 18, 2011, 1447–51; Kirsten Weir, "Revising Your

Story," *Monitor on Psychology*/American Psychological Association 43, no. 3 (March 2012): 28.

99   *"What's the harm?"*: Author interview, as broadcast on National Public Radio, "Editing Your Life's Stories Can Create Happier Endings," Jan. 1, 2014, https://www.npr.org/templates/transcript/transcript.php?storyId=258674011.

100   *Mary Poppins bag*: Lauren Alloy and C. M. Clements, "Illusion of Control: Invulnerability to Negative Affect and Depressive Symptoms after Laboratory and Natural Stressors," *Journal of Abnormal Psychology* 101, no. 2 (May 1992): 234–45; Sandra Murray and John Holmes, "The Self-Fulfilling Nature of Positive Illusions in Romantic Relationships: Love Is Not Blind, but Prescient," *Journal of Personality and Social Psychology* 71, no. 6 (1996): 1155–80; Taylor and Brown, "Illusion and Well-Being," 193–210.

100   *even better physical health*: Judith Rodin and Ellen Langer, "Long-term Effects of a Control-Relevant Intervention with the Institutionalized Aged," *Journal of Personality and Social Psychology* 35, no. 12 (1977): 897.

100   *prescribed in psychologists' offices*: Brad J. Bushman and Roy F. Baumeister, "Threatened Egotism, Narcissism, Self-Esteem, and Direct and Displaced Aggression: Does Self-Love or Self-Hate Lead to Violence?," *Journal of Personality and Social Psychology* 75, no. 1 (1998): 219.

100   *"considerable evidence suggests positive psychological benefits"*: National Institute of Mental Health Report, 1995, 182, as cited in Richard W. Robins and Jennifer S. Beer, "Positive Illusions About the Self: Short-Term Benefits and Long-Term Costs," *Journal of Personality and Social Psychology* 80, no. 2 (2001): 340.

100   *wondered why some of her students seemed to struggle*: Angela Duckworth, personal website, https://angeladuckworth.com/media/.

101   *"extremely long-term objectives"*: Angela Duckworth, Christopher Peterson, Michael D. Matthews, and Dennis R. Kelly, "Grit: Perseverance and Passion for Long-Term Goals," *Journal of Personality and Social Psychology* 92, no. 6 (2007): 1089.

101   *Musicians. Athletes. Chefs*: Angela Duckworth, *Grit: The Power of Passion and Perseverance* (New York: Scribner, 2016), 57, 74–78.

101   *what cognitive glitch helps you achieve grit? Positive illusions*: Erin Marie O'Mara and Lowell Gaertner, "Does Self-Enhancement Facilitate Task Performance?" *Journal of Experimental Psychology: General* 146, no. 3 (2017): 442–55; Richard B. Felson, "The Effect of Self-Appraisals of Ability on Academic Performance," *Journal of Personality and Social Psychology* 47, no. 5 (1984): 944–52.

101   *less likely to experience discouragement after setbacks*: Alloy and Clements, "Illusion of Control"; Taylor and Brown, "Illusion and Well-Being"; S. Thompson, "Illusions of Control: How We Overestimate Our Personal Influence," *Current Directions in Psychological Science* 8 (1999): 187–90; Numerous studies cited in Dufner, "Self-Enhancement and Psychological Adjustment," 51.

101   *"maintaining effort"*: Duckworth et al., "Grit: Perseverance and Passion for Long-Term Goals," 1087–88.

102 *"I became accustomed to work persistently"*: Jordan, *The Days of a Man, Volume One*, 46.

102 *the Botany Prize . . . the Entomology Prize . . . the French History Prize*: Ibid., 75–76.

102 *he had a knack for slyly editing out or omitting information*: Author interview, June 18, 2019.

102 *"sexual perversity!"*: Carnochan, "The Case of Julius Goebel: Stanford, 1905," 99.

103 *"trunk . . . full of applications for positions in the faculty"*: David Starr Jordan, as quoted in Bailey Millard, "Jordan of Stanford," *Los Angeles Times Sunday Magazine*, Jan. 21, 1934, 6.

103 *"Every age gets the lunatics it deserves"*: Roy Porter, "Reason, Madness, and the French Revolution," *Studies in Eighteenth-Century Culture* 20 (1991): 73.

103 *Delroy Paulhus found*: Delroy Paulhus, "Interpersonal and Intrapsychic Adaptiveness of Trait Self-Enhancement: A Mixed Blessing," *Journal of Personality and Social Psychology* 74, no. 5 (1998): 1197–1208.

104 *overconfidence has serious costs in the workplace*: Tomas Chamorro-Premuzic, *Confidence: The Surprising Truth About How Much You Really Need and How to Get It* (London: Profile Books Ltd, 2013).

104 *One of the most widely cited studies*: James Coyne, "Re-examining Ellen Langer's Classic Study of Giving Plants to Nursing Home Residents," *Coyne of the Realm*, Nov. 5, 2014, http://www.coyneoftherealm.com/2014/11/05/re-examining-ellen-langers-classic-study-giving-plants-nursing-home-residents/; Judith Rodin and Ellen Langer, "Erratum to Rodin and Langer," *Journal of Personality and Social Psychology* 36, no. 5 (1978): 462.

104 *well-regarded in a community*: Dufner, "Self-Enhancement and Psychological Adjustment," 63, 66.

104 *depressive counterparts*: Wilberta L. Donovan, "Maternal Self-Efficacy: Illusory Control and Its Effect on Susceptibility to Learned Helplessness," *Child Development* 61, no. 5 (Oct. 1990): 1638–47.

104 *"short-term benefits but long-term costs"*: Richard W. Robins and Jennifer S. Beer, "Short-Term Benefits and Long-Term Costs," *Journal of Personality and Social Psychology* 80, no. 2 (2001): 341.

105 *"low self-esteem underlies aggression"*: Bushman and Baumeister, "Threatened Egotism," 219.

105 *insulted them, and waited to see who would lash out*: Ibid., 222.

105 *people with a grandiose view of themselves who strike out*: Ibid., 219, 223.

105 *"Aggressors often think very highly of themselves"*: Ibid., 219.

105 *Fidel Castro once proposed building a shield*: Abey Obejas and David Greene, "Complicated Feelings: 'The Little Fidel in All of Us,'" *Morning Edition*, National Public Radio, Nov. 30, 2016, http://www.npr.org/2016/11/30/503825310/complicated-feelings-the-little-fidel-in-all-of-us.

105 *Yury Luzhkov wanted to stop snowfall*: Joshua Keating, "Moscow to ban snow," *Foreign Policy*, Oct. 15, 2009, https://foreignpolicy.com/2009/10/15/moscow-to-ban-snow/.

106 *"physically imposing"*: United States Government Accountability Office, "Report to Congressional Requesters," July 2018, 19, https://www.gao.gov/assets/700/693488.pdf.

106 *concrete or steel*: JM Rieger, "For years Trump promised to build a wall from concrete. Now he says it will be built from steel," *Washington Post*, Jan. 7, 2019, https://www.washingtonpost.com/politics/2019/01/07/years-trump-promised-build-wall-concrete-now-he-says-it-will-be-built-steel/.

106 *"In plainer terms"*: Bushman and Baumeister, "Threatened Egotism," 228.

106 *"Jordan's most double-edged talents"*: Spoehr, "Freedom to Do Right," 53.

Chapter 9: The Bitterest Thing in the World

109 *"whitewashing" a sex scandal*: Goebel to Stanford, June 6, 1904 (Stanford Archives, Horace Davis Papers SC0028, Box 1, Folder 10), as cited in Carnochan, "The Case of Julius Goebel: Stanford, 1905," 99.

109 *rumors were flying that Jane was about to fire him*: Spoehr, "Progress' Pilgrim," 138.

109 *"queer" and "bitter"*: Cutler, *The Mysterious Death of Jane Stanford*, 20–25.

109 *clearing everybody*: Ibid., 25.

110 *"the most murderous hatred of all"*: Ibid., 32–33.

110 *Jane set sail for Hawaii*: Ibid., 9–10, 23, 98.

110 *According to weather data*: US Department of Agriculture, "Report for February 1905: Hawaiian Section of the Climate and Crop Service of the Weather Bureau," 7, https://babel.hathitrust.org/cgi/pt?id=uc1.$c188080&view=1up&seq=23.

110 *gingerbread, hard-boiled eggs, meat-and-cheese sandwiches*: Pacific Commercial Advertiser, March 2, 1905, as cited in Cutler, *The Mysterious Death of Jane Stanford*, 10.

110 *For a few hours, they sat in the shade*: Cutler, *The Mysterious Death of Jane Stanford*, 9.

110 *had a light dinner of soup*: Ibid., 10.

110 *"Bertha! May!" Jane called. "I am so sick!"*: Ibid., 12.

111 *He sat with Jane, gently palpating her jaw*: Ibid., 12–13.

111 *"Oh God, forgive me my sins"*: Ibid., 14.

111 *She was dead, only fifteen minutes after it had all begun*: Ibid.

111 *stomach pump dangling uselessly from his hand*: Ibid.

111 *noted a foreign, bitter taste*: Ibid., 15.

111 *sent Jane's body to the morgue*: Ibid.

111 *convulsions and lockjaw*: Ibid., 17.

111 *watching them recoil*: Ibid., 17–18.

111 *traces of strychnine in both*: Ibid., 39–41.

112 *the bright red indicative of strychnine*: Ibid., 41.

112 *hard white octahedral crystals*: Ibid., 39–40.

112 *seasoned physician*: Ibid., 11.

112 *far more extreme than rigor mortis*: Ibid., 17–18.

112 *"a condition that I don't recall having seen"*: Ibid., 15.

112 *"felonious intent by some person or persons to this jury unknown"*: Ibid., 45.

112 *"nothing whatever to do with the investigation"*: "Quick Stanford Verdict," *New York Times*, March 11, 1905.

112 *The man David selected*: Cutler, *The Mysterious Death of Jane Stanford*, 47.

113 *What concerned him was the* amount *of strychnine*: Ibid., 48; "Testimony of Dr. Water-house," Stanford University Archives, as cited in Cutler, *The Mysterious Death of Jane Stanford*, 48, 55.

113 *transformed into a grotesque feast of rancid gingerbread*: Cutler, *The Mysterious Death of Jane Stanford*, 46, 62.

113 *Jane then sucked down* eight *sandwiches*: Ibid., 62.

113 *"morally certain"*: Jordan to Carl S. Smith, Mar. 24, 1905, Special Collections and University Archives, Stanford University, SC0033B, Series 4, Box 1, Folder 11, 4, https://purl.stanford.edu/dr431vh4868.

113 *"wholly convinced"*; *"a surfeit of unsuitable food"*: "Not Murder, Says Jordan: Thinks Unfit Food and Exertion Killed Mrs. Stanford," *New York Times*, March 15, 1905.

114 *"eleven hours later?"*: Author interview, Feb. 8, 2017. All further remarks of Dr. Yasmin's are from this conversation.

115 *"scarcely earned"*: Jordan, *The Days of a Man, Volume One*, 146.

115 *"more sure than ever that she was not poisoned"*: "Jordan Scouts Poison Idea: University President Doesn't Think Mrs. Stanford Was Murdered," *New York Times*, March 15, 1905.

115 *explained it away as "medicinal"*: "Not Murder, Says Jordan: Thinks Unfit Food and Exertion Killed Mrs. Stanford."

116 *a most logical explanation: "hysteria"*: Cutler, *The Mysterious Death of Jane Stanford*, 50.

116 *On his final morning on the island*: Ibid., 54.

116 *He scribbled down a few words*: Ibid., 56.

116 *"generous-hearted," "helpful and sympathetic"*: "Not Murder, Says Jordan: Thinks Unfit Food and Exertion Killed Mrs. Stanford."

116 *He then signed the statement*: Cutler, *The Mysterious Death of Jane Stanford*, 55.

116 *one of her pallbearers*: Ibid., 54.

117 *"She did not die of angina pectoris"*: *Pacific Commercial Advertiser*, March 17, 1905, as cited in Cutler, *The Mysterious Death of Jane Stanford*, 56.

117 *"a man without professional or personal standing"*: Jordan to Judge Samuel Franklin Leib, March 22, 1905, Stanford University Archives, as cited in Cutler, *The Mysterious Death of Jane Stanford*, 37. Leib succeeded Jane Stanford as president of the Stanford University board of trustees.

117 *David accused them all of colluding in a conspiracy*: Cutler, *The Mysterious Death of Jane Stanford*, 75–76.

117 *"never conclusively determined"*: "Jane Stanford: The Woman Behind Stanford University," Stanford University website, July 17, 2010, https://web.archive.org/web/20160521025646/http://janestanford.stanford.edu/biography.html.

117 *"died under mysterious circumstances"*: "Meet President Jordan," *Stanford Magazine*, January 2010, https://stanfordmag.org/contents/meet-president-jordan.

118 *Robert was shocked*: Lee Romney, "The Alma Mater Mystery," *Los Angeles Times*, October 10, 2003.

118 *He had advanced emphysema*: Maggie Cutler, author interview, May 12, 2017.

119 *Robert Cutler won't wager a guess*: Cutler, *The Mysterious Death of Jane Stanford*, 104–8.

119 *"had the motive"*: Carnochan, "The Case of Julius Goebel: Stanford, 1905," 108.

119 *White's current guess is that Bertha did it*: Author interview, Richard White, May 11, 2017.

119 *possible to die from eating too much food*: Fred(?) Baker to David Starr Jordan, March 4, 1905, Special Collections and University Archives, Stanford University, SC0033B, Series 4, Box 1, Folder 14.

119 *his "silence can't be bought"*: Goebel to Jordan, May 24, 1905, Special Collections and University Archives, Stanford University, SC0058, Series IB, Box 47, Folder 194.

119 *"judged in the afterlife"*: Unknown to Jordan, March 16, 1905, Special Collections and University Archives, Stanford University, SC0033B, Series 4, Box 1, Folder 14; see also Special Collections and University Archives, Stanford University, SC0058, Series IAA, Box 14, Vol. 28 for two letters regarding Dr. Waterhouse being accused of unethical behavior: Jordan to Mountford Wilson, May 10, 1905 (it is mentioned that the other Hawaii doctors are going to write about Dr. Waterhouse's poor conduct in a medical journal); Jordan to Waterhouse, May 4, 1905 (Jordan assures Dr. Waterhouse he acted appropriately).

119 *David's continuing to insist that Jane had died of natural causes*: Author interview, Richard White, May 11, 2017.

120 *A duty to unearth a truth*: Author interview, Maggie Cutler, May 12, 2017.

120 *"He absolutely believed that Jordan did it"*: Author interview, Maggie Cutler, April 14, 2017.

121 *"The doctor needed a villain"*: Author interview, April 2017.

121 *cross from speculation to "fantasy"*: Luther Spoehr, "Letters to the Editor," *Stanford Magazine*, March/Apr. 2004, https://stanfordmag.org/contents/letters-to-the-editor -8521.

122 *devil's horns*: Drawings, Special Collections and University Archives, Stanford University, SC0058, Series IV-C, Box 6B, Folder 25.

122 *a small rectangular notecard*: Lathrop to Jordan, March 1905, Special Collections and University Archives, Stanford University, SC0058, Series IA, Box 46, Folder 451.

122 *the killer is still on the loose*: Newspaper clipping (paper unknown), "Dr. Jordan's Statement Is Riddled by the Experts," Special Collections and University Archives, Stanford University, SC0058, Series IA, Box 46, Folder 451.

122 *Jessie calling David the "miracle" of her life*: Jessie Knight handwritten remembrance, Special Collections and University Archives, Stanford University, SC0058, Series I-F, Box 6, Folder 48.

122 *medallions he won for advocating peace*: Box of medals, Special Collections and University Archives, Stanford University, SC0058, Series XI, Box 7.

122   *"the killing business"*: David Starr Jordan, "Where Uncle Sam's Solar Plexus Is Located," unknown newspaper, Apr. 1915, David Starr Jordan papers, Box 53, Folder 28, Hoover Institution Archives.

123   *caterpillars, spiders, leaves:* Journals, Special Collections and University Archives, Stanford University, SC0058, Series IIA, Box 1.

123   *"the old 'swimming hole' or the deep eddy at the root of the old stump"*: David Starr Jordan, *A Guide to the Study of Fishes* (New York: Henry Holt and Company, 1905), 3.

123   *"the bitterest thing in the world"*: Judge George E. Crothers to Cora (Mrs. Fremont) Older, Jan. 10, 1905, Stanford University Archives, as cited in Cutler, *The Mysterious Death of Jane Stanford*, 104.

123   *Strychnine:* Jordan, *A Guide to the Study of Fishes*, 430.

Chapter 10: A Veritable Chamber of Horrors

127   *The erosion of David Starr Jordan's:* Luther Spoehr, "Freedom to Do Right," 17–24, 28–31, 36.

127   *in 1913 . . . chancellor:* "Meet President Jordan," *Stanford Magazine.*

127   *His travels as a fish collector:* Jordan, *The Days of a Man, Volume Two*, 314–15.

128   *"a veritable chamber of horrors"*: David Starr Jordan, *The Human Harvest: A Study of the Decay of Races Through the Survival of the Unfit* (Boston: American Unitarian Association, 1907), 64–65.

128   *immobile creatures:* Jordan, *Foot-Notes to Evolution*, 277–78.

128   *"animal pauperism"*: Ibid., 279.

128   *"new species of man"*: Jordan, *The Days of a Man, Volume Two*, 314.

128   *"the survival of the unfittest"*: Jordan, *The Human Harvest*, 54, 62.

128   *extermination:* Ibid., 65.

128   *"crétins"*: Ibid., 63–65.

128   *"decay"*: Ibid., 34, 49, 69; David Starr Jordan, *The Blood of the Nation: A Study of the Decay of Races Through the Survival of the Unfit* (Boston: American Unitarian Association, 1906).

129   *"epoch in my own mental development"*: Francis Galton, *Memories of my Life* (London: Methuen, 1909), as cited in Nicholas Gillham, "Cousins: Charles Darwin, Sir Francis Galton, and the Birth of Eugenics," The Royal Statistical Society, Aug. 24, 2009, 133, https://rss.onlinelibrary.wiley.com/doi/full/10.1111/j.1740-9713.2009.00379.x.

129   *He trotted out his ideas:* Gillham, "Cousins: Charles Darwin, Sir Francis Galton, and the Birth of Eugenics," 134.

129   *He even wrote a sci-fi novel:* Francis Galton, *The Eugenic College of Kantsaywhere*, University College London, Galton Collection, 28–29, 45–47; see also Francis Galton and Lyman Tower Sargent, "The Eugenic College of Kantsaywhere," *Utopian Studies* 12, no. 2 (2001).

129   *"sharp severity"*: Galton, *Kantsaywhere*, 45–47.

129   *"attached so exaggerated an importance"*: Burns, *David Starr Jordan: Prophet of Freedom*, 37.

129   *decades before most American eugenicists got the fever*: Jordan, *The Days of a Man, Volume One*, 132–33.

130   *traits like "pauperism" and "degener[acy]"*: Jordan, *Evolution: Syllabus of Lectures* (Alameda, CA, 1892), 9, Special Collections and University Archives, Stanford University, SC0058, Series IIB, Box 7.

130   *"exterminated just as swamps are drained"*: Ibid.

130   *"as long as the human harvest is good"*: Jordan, *The Human Harvest*, 6; see "Prefatory Note," 5: "This little book contains the substance of two essays on the same subject, the one originally delivered in Stanford University in 1899 . . . the other read at Philadelphia in 1906, at the two hundredth anniversary of the birth of Benjamin Franklin."

130   *first pro-eugenics article in 1898*: Jordan, *Foot-Notes to Evolution*.

130   *"crétins" and "imbeciles"*: Jordan, *The Human Harvest*, 62–65.

130   *stops at churches and almshouses*: Ibid., 64–65; various news clippings ("David Starr Jordan Speaks Here Tonight," "That Japanese Bugaboo") found in Special Collections and University Archives, Stanford University, SC0058, Series III, Box 4, Volume 6.

130   *"the survival of the unfit"*: Jordan, *The Human Harvest*, 62–63.

130   *"goitered" . . . "creatures"*: Jordan, *The Days of a Man, Volume Two*, 314–15.

130   *He had sketches made*: Jordan, *Foot-Notes to Evolution*, 285–86.

130   *Others suggested legalizing polygamy*: Harry H. Laughlin, "Eugenics Record Office; Bulletin No. 10A; Report of the Committee to Study and to Report on the Best Practical Means of Cutting Off the Defective Germ-Plasm in the American Population," *National Information Resource on Ethics and Human Genetics* (Feb. 1914): 46.

131   *"each individual cretin should be the last of his generation"*: Jordan, *The Human Harvest*, 65.

131   *In 1915, a doctor in Chicago*: "Surgeon Lets Baby, Born to Idiocy, Die," *New York Times*, July 15, 1917.

131   *"the Black Stork"*: *The Black Stork*, written by Jack Lait and Harry Haiselden, dir. Leopold Wharton and Theodore Wharton, Sheriott Pictures Corp., Feb. 1917.

131   *rumors of a mental hospital*: Edwin Black, "Eugenics and the Nazis—the California Connection," *San Francisco Chronicle*, Nov. 9, 2003, https://www.sfgate.com/opinion/article/Eugenics-and-the-Nazis-the-California-2549771.php.

131   *a handful of doctors*: Author interview, Paul A. Lombardo, Aug. 27, 2019.

131   *the "quiet way"*: Paul A. Lombardo, *Three Generations, No Imbeciles: Eugenics, the Supreme Court, and Buck v. Bell* (Baltimore: Johns Hopkins University Press, 2008), 22, citing "Whipping and Castrations as Punishments for Crime," *Yale Law Journal*, vol. 8, June 1899, 382.

131   *first such law not just in the country but in the world*: Lombardo, *Three Generations, No Imbeciles*, 24; 1907 Indiana Laws, ch. 215; Lutz Kaelbor, "Presentation about 'Eugenic Sterilizations' in Comparative Perspective at the 2012 Social Science History Association," https://www.uvm.edu/~lkaelber/eugenics/IN/IN.html.

131   *he was asked to chair*: Elof Axel Carlson, *The Unfit: A History of a Bad Idea* (Cold Spring Harbor, NY: Cold Spring Harbor Laboratory Press, 2001), 193.

131   *it crossed party lines*: Author interview with Paul Lombardo, Apr. 30, 2019.

131   *prestigious universities all across the country*: Adam S. Cohen, "Harvard's Eugenics Era," *Harvard Magazine*, March 2016.

132   *the fairest skin, the roundest head, the most symmetrical features*: Alexandra Minna Stern, "Making Better Babies: Public Health and Race Betterment in Indiana, 1920–1935," *American Journal of Public Health* 92, no. 5 (May 2002): 748, 750.

132   *American eugenicist named Madison Grant*: Madison Grant, *The Passing of the Great Race: Or the Racial Basis of European Ancestry* (New York: Charles Scribner's Sons, 1916).

132   *Hitler would later call his "bible"*: Stefan Kühl, *The Nazi Connection: Eugenics, American Racism, and German National Socialism* (Oxford: Oxford University Press, 2002), 85; Timothy Ryback, "A Disquieting Book from Hitler's Library," *New York Times*, Dec. 7, 2011.

132   *"moral perverts, mental defectives and hereditary cripples"*: Grant, *The Passing of the Great Race*, 45.

132   *rounded up under the guise of charity and sterilized*: Ibid., 45–51.

132   *"The Germans are beating us at our own game"*: Edwin Black, "The Horrifying American Roots of Nazi Eugenics," History News Network, Sept. 2003, http://historynews network.org/article/1796.

132   *American Bar Association called eugenic sterilization "barbari[c]"*: Lombardo, *Three Generations, No Imbeciles*, 58.

132   *"an engine of tyranny and oppression"*: Portland lawyer C. E. S. Wood, as cited in Lombardo, *Three Generations, No Imbeciles*, 28.

133   *"To permit such an operation"*: Governor Samuel Pennypacker, as cited in David R. Berman, *Governors and the Progressive Movement* (Louisville, CO: University Press of Colorado, 2019), 184.

133   *"rot"*: Lombardo, *Three Generations, No Imbeciles*, 28.

133   *Darwin hails the power of "Variation"*: Darwin, *On the Origin of Species*, 26, 36, 61, 63, 66, 74, 90, 107, 168, 204, 216, 304.

133   *He marvels over how diverse gene pools are healthier*: Ibid., 26, 61, 63, 66, 72, 168, 204.

133   *gives more "vigor and fertility"*: Ibid., 168.

133   *"How strange are these facts!"*: Ibid., 63.

134   *"Diversify your genetic portfolio"*: Ibid., 26, 66, 168.

134   *Darwin even goes out of his way to warn against meddling*: Ibid., 79–80.

134   *"abhorrent to our ideas of fitness"*: Ibid., 296.

134   *"Man can act only on external and visible characters"*: Ibid., 53.

134   *the case of the cyanobacteria*: Elizabeth Pennisi, "Meet the obscure microbe that influences climate, ocean ecosystems, and perhaps even evolution," *Science*, March 9, 2017, https://www.sciencemag.org/news/2017/03/meet-obscure-microbe-influences -climate-ocean-ecosystems-and-perhaps-even-evolution.

134   *"Which group will prevail"*: Darwin, *On the Origin of Species*, 79–80.

134 *"dandelion principle"*: Thorkil Sonne, as quoted in David Bornstein, "For Some with Autism, Jobs to Match Their Talents," *New York Times*, June 30, 2011.

134 *"indispensable"*: Darwin, *Origin of Species*, 63.

135 *naïve, sentimental*: Jordan, *The Human Harvest*, 62–65; Grant, *The Passing of the Great Race*, 49.

135 *"[E]ducation can never replace heredity"*: David Starr Jordan, *Your Family Tree* (New York: D. Appleton and Co, 1929), 10.

135 *"An Arab proverb"*: Ibid., 5.

135 *to give over half a million dollars*: Harry Laughlin, "Notes of the History of the Eugenics Record Office," Dec. 31, 1939, Private Collection, Eugenics Record Office; Jordan, *The Days of a Man, Volume Two*, 297–98; Lombardo, *Three Generations, No Imbeciles*, 31.

135 *construct family trees*: Kaaren Norrgard, "Human Testing, the Eugenics Movement, and IRBs," *Nature Education* 1, no. 1 (2008): 170, https://www.nature.com/scitable /topicpage/human-testing-the-eugenics-movement-and-irbs-724.

135 *"thalassophilia"*: Charles Davenport, as cited in Garland E. Allen, "The Eugenics Record Office at Cold Spring Harbor, 1910–1940: An Essay in Institutional History," *Osiris* 2 (1986): 225–64.

135 *inheritance of albinism and neurofibromatosis*: Norrgard, "Human Testing, the Eugenics Movement, and IRBs."

135 *unequivocally debunked*: Ibid.

136 *"palpable inhumanity and immorality"*: Lombardo, *Three Generations, No Imbeciles*, 27.

136 *"man-crazy"*: Ibid., 61.

136 *"I am a humanbeen as well as you"*: Letter from George Mallory to Albert Priddy, Nov. 5, 1917. Record, *Mallory v. Priddy*, as cited in Lombardo, *Three Generations, No Imbeciles*, 70.

136 *began searching for a case*: Lombardo, *Three Generations, No Imbeciles*, 91–110; "A. S. Priddy Summons" (2009), *Buck v. Bell Documents*, Paper 17, http://readingroom.law .gsu.edu/buckvbell/17.

136 *Dr. Priddy found*: Lombardo, *Three Generations, No Imbeciles*, 103–12.

137 *he had Carrie's baby*: Ibid., 111.

137 *likely running a coin*: Paul Lombardo, "Facing Carrie Buck," *Hastings Center Report* 33, no. 2 (March 2003): 16, https://doi.org/10.2307/3528148.

137 *"showed backwardness"*: Arthur Estabrook testimony, *Buck v. Priddy*, Amherst, VA, 1924, as cited in http://www.eugenicsarchive.org/html/eugenics/static/themes/39 .html.

137 *A lawyer named Irving Whitehead*: Ibid., 107–8, 115, 117, 135, 136–48, 155.

137 *his vision was going; he had developed diabetes*: Burns, *David Starr Jordan*, 32–33; Jordan, *The Days of a Man, Volume One*, 45.

137 *grown into a paleontologist*: "Eric Jordan Hurt In Auto Accident Near Gilroy Today," *Stanford Daily*, March 10, 1926, https://stanforddailyarchive.com/cgi-bin /stanford?a=d&d=stanford19260310-01.2.17&e=-------en-20--1--txt-txIN-------.

137 "*moral delinquency*": ERO's Harry Laughlin testimony, *Buck v. Priddy*, Amherst, VA, 1924, as cited in https://www.facinghistory.org/resource-library/supreme-court-and -sterilization-carrie-buck.

138 "*No, sir, I have not*": *Buck Record*, 33–35, as cited in Lombardo, *Three Generations, No Imbeciles*, 107.

138 "*swamped with incompetence*": *Buck v. Bell*, 274 US 200 (1927).

138 *a skylight provided extra light for the surgeon*: Carolyn Robinson (Training and Policy Director at the Central Virginia Training Center), as reported to *Encyclopedia Virginia* reporter Miranda Bennett, 2018.

138 *sealed each cut with carbolic acid*: Paul Lombardo, "In the Letters of an 'Imbecile,' the Sham, and Shame, of Eugenics," *UnDark*, Oct. 4, 2017, https://undark.org/article /carrie-buck-letters-eugenics/.

138 "*They done me wrong*": quoted in Adam Cohen, *Imbeciles: The Supreme Court, American Eugenics, and the Sterilization of Carrie Buck* (New York: Penguin Press, 2016), 298.

138 "*public welfare*": *Buck v. Bell*, 274 US 200 (1927).

138 *a set of microfilm reels*: Sarah Zhang, "A Long-Lost Data Trove Uncovers California's Sterilization Program," *Atlantic*, Jan. 3, 2017, https://www.theatlantic.com/health /archive/2017/01/california-sterilization-records/511718/.

139 *The list was nearly 20,000 people long*: Alexandra Minna Stern, "When California Sterilized 20,000 of Its Citizens," *Zocalo*, Jan. 6, 2016, http://www.zocalopublicsquare .org/2016/01/06/when-california-sterilized-20000-of-its-citizens/chronicles/who -we-were/.

139 "*often were young women pronounced promiscuous*": Ibid.

139 *women of color were disproportionately targeted*: Nicole L. Novak, Natalie Lira, Kate E. O'Connor, Siobán D. Harlow, Sharon L. Kardia, and Alexandra Minna Stern, "Disproportionate Sterilization of Latinos Under California's Eugenic Sterilization Program, 1920–1945," *American Journal of Public Health* 108 (May 2018): 611–13, https://doi.org/10.2105/AJPH.2018.304369.

139 *sterilizing over 2,500 Native American women*: Carolyn Hoemann, "Genuine Justice: Sterilization Abuse of Native American Women," KRUI, Oct. 17, 2016, http://krui .fm/2016/10/17/genuine-justice-sterilization-abuse-native-american-women/.

139 *sterilized hundreds of black women*: Lutz Kaelber, "Eugenics/Sexual Sterilizations in North Carolina," University of Vermont website, https://www.uvm.edu/~lkaelber/eu genics/NC/NC.html.

139 *approximately a third of all Puerto Rican women*: "Puerto Rico," Eugenics Archive, http://eugenicsarchive.ca/discover/connections/530ba18176f0db569b00001b.

139 *words like "mentally incompetent" or "mentally deficient"*: Georgia Code Ann. § 31-20-3 (West), https://law.justia.com/codes/georgia/2010/title-31/chapter-20/31-20-3/; New Jersey, Stat. Ann. § 30:6D-5 (West), https://law.justia.com/codes/new-jersey/2013 /title-30/section-30-6d-5/.

140 *nearly 150 women were illegally sterilized in California prisons*: Corey G. Johnson, "Fe-

male Inmates Sterilized in California Prisons Without Approval," Reveal from The Center for Investigative Reporting, July 7, 2013, https://www.revealnews.org/article/female-inmates-sterilized-in-california-prisons-without-approval/.

140 *Tennessee judge named Sam Benningfield*: Derek Hawkins, "Tenn. Judge Reprimanded for Offering Reduced Jail Time in Exchange for Sterilization," *Washington Post*, Nov. 11, 2017.

140 *Francis Galton, in bronze*: Lombardo, *Three Generations, No Imbeciles*, 101; "Chapter Two—Exterior Stone Carvings and Bronze Work," National Academy of Sciences website, http://www.nasonline.org/about-nas/visiting-nas/nas-building/exterior-carvings-and-bronze.html.

Chapter 11: The Ladder

143 *"hidden and insignificant"*: Jordan, *The Days of a Man, Volume One*, 25.

143 *"a terrifying capacity"*: Spoehr, "Progress' Pilgrim," 216.

144 *"His ability to crush those in his path"*: Spoehr, "Freedom to Do Right," 53.

144 *"missionary work of the highest order"*: Jordan, *The Days of a Man, Volume One*, 111.

145 *"I just wish he had considered what Oliver Cromwell once said"*: Author interview, Luther Spoehr, June 18, 2019.

145 *wrote them off as sentimental, unscientific*: Jordan, *Your Family Tree*, 4–5, 9–10.

146 *There are crows that have better memories than us*: Robert Krulwich, "How a 5-Ounce Bird Stores 10,000 Maps in Its Head," *National Geographic*, Dec. 3, 2015.

146 *chimps with better pattern-recognition skills*: Sana Inoue and Tetsuro Matsuzawa, "Working Memory of Numerals in Chimpanzees," *Current Biology*, Dec. 2007.

146 *ants that rescue their wounded*: Elise Nowbahari and Karen L. Hollis, "Rescue Behavior: Distinguishing Between Rescue, Cooperation and Other Forms of Altruistic Behavior," *Communicative & Integrative Biology* 3, no. 2 (2010): 77–9, doi:10.4161/cib.3.2.10018.

146 *blood flukes with higher rates of monogamy*: Michelle Steinauer, "The Sex Lives of Parasites: Investigating the Mating System and Mechanisms of Sexual Selection of the Human Pathogen Schistosoma Mansoni," *International Journal for Parasitology*, Aug. 2009, 1157–63.

146 Natura non facit saltum: Darwin, *On the Origin of Species*, 288, 295.

146 *a parasite was not an abomination but a marvel*: Ibid., 39. Interestingly, shortly after *Origin of Species* was published, Darwin changed his tune, at least about one parasite. He wrote to Asa Gray saying the horror of the parasitic wasp, *Ichneumonidae*, made him question his faith: "I cannot persuade myself that a beneficent and omnipotent God would have designedly created the Ichneumonidae." Darwin to Gray, May 22, 1860, Darwin Correspondence Project, http://www.darwinproject.ac.uk/letter/DCP-LETT-2814.xml.

146 *endless ways of surviving and thriving in this world*: Ibid., 39, 296.

Chapter 12: Dandelions

151 *close its doors*: Governor Bob McDonnell, as quoted in "CVTC Closing as Part of Department of Justice Agreement," ABC 13 News, Jan. 26, 2012, https://wset.com/archive /cvtc-closing-as-part-of-department-of-justice-agreement.

152 *tend cows, hogs, and various crops at a profit*: "History," Central Virginia Training Center, http://www.cvtc.dbhds.virginia.gov/feedback.htm.

152 *over a thousand graves*: "Central Virginia Training Center Cemetery," Central Virginia Training Center, http://www.cvtc.dbhds.virginia.gov/cemeter.htm.

152 *The very mind-set we define our national identity in opposition to*: Lombardo, *Three Generations, No Imbeciles*, 239.

153 *honor roll at the local elementary school*: Lombardo, *Three Generations*, 190–91.

153 *"I think about it every day, though"*: Author interview, Anna, March 7, 2017.

153 *The year was 1967*: Department of Mental Hygiene and Hospitals Sterilization Record Summary, 1967, Anna's personal documents.

153 *inside its brick walls twelve years earlier*: Author interview, Anna, March 7, 2017.

154 *people dying on the operating table*: Author interview, Anna, June 8, 2018.

155 *"I told her don't worry"*: Ibid.

155 *not sure how she would have survived*: Ibid.

155 *Then, on a muggy August day in 1967*: Acute Hospital Discharge Summary, Aug. 9, 1967, Anna's personal documents; Cenon Q. Baltazar, letter to Daisy, Aug. 3, 1967, Anna's personal documents.

156 *"They told Anna she couldn't take care of kids"*: Author interview, June 8, 2018.

157 *she felt angry*: Ibid.

160 *"Because of me!"*: Ibid.

161 *"those are my sweethearts!"*: Author interview, May 23, 2018.

162 *"whole machinery of life"*: Darwin, *On the Origin of Species*, 304.

162 *The work of good science is to try to peer beyond*: Ibid., 79–80, 293–6, 301–2, 304–5.

Chapter 13: Deus ex Machina

167 *surrounded by his menagerie of loved ones*: "Dr. David Starr Jordan Dies," *Healdsburg Tribune*, Sept. 19, 1931.

167 *"the great humanitarian's garden"*: *Daily Palo Alto Times*, Oct. 4, 1934 (as found in Special Collections and University Archives, Stanford University, SC0058, Series I-F, Box 6).

168 *"Few men have lived lives more balanced"*: Burns, *David Starr Jordan: Prophet of Freedom*, 33.

168 *"one of the most versatile"*: Ibid., 1.

168 *a German general who commanded, "Genug!"*: Elof Axel Carlson, *The Unfit: A History of a Bad Idea* (Cold Spring Harbor, NY: Cold Spring Harbor Laboratory Press, 2001), 193.

168 *"the best it breeds to destruction"*: Jordan, *The Human Harvest*, 51.

169 *More than four thousand feet above sea level*: Mount Jordan, a 4,067-meter peak in Tuolumne County, California.

169 *two high schools*: David Starr Jordan High School in Los Angeles, CA; David Jordan High School in Long Beach, CA.

169 *a government ship*: NOAAS *David Starr Jordan* (R 444) in commission from 1966 to 2010, www.noaa.gov.

169 *a city boulevard*: Jordan Avenue in Bloomington, Indiana.

169 *one in Alaska*: Jordan Lake, near the Naha River. Jordan, *The Days of a Man, Volume Two*, 138.

169 *one in Utah*: Mount Jordan in Duchesne County, Utah.

169 *a prestigious scientific award*: "The David Starr Jordan Prize for Innovative Contributions to the Study of Evolution, Ecology, Population, or Organismal Biology," Cornell University, http://www.indiana.edu/~dsjprize/index.html.

169 *of the 12,000–13,000 species*: Jordan, *The Days of a Man, Volume One*, 288.

169 *Recent scholarship by Jessica George*: Jessica George, "The Immigrants Who Supplied the Smithsonian's Fish Collection," *Edge Effects*, Nov. 7, 2017, https://edgeeffects.net /fish-collection/.

169 *a "small boy"*: Jordan, *Guide to the Study of Fishes*, 430.

169 *"half-breed"*: Jordan, *The Days of a Man, Volume One*, 533.

169 *"Portuguese lad"*: Ibid., 211.

169 *"Of the hundred or more new species"*: Jordan, *Guide to the Study of Fishes*, 430.

170 *"few to none"*: George S. Meyers, foreword to David Starr Jordan's *The Genera of Fishes and A Classification of Fishes* (Stanford, CA: Stanford University Press, 1963), xv.

170 *"impact of David Starr Jordan has been so pervasive"*: Theodore W. Pietsch and William D. Anderson, *Collection Building in Ichthyology and Herpetology* (Lawrence, KS: American Society of Ichthyologists, 1997), 5.

171 *"The Death of the Fish"*: Yoon, *Naming Nature*, 239.

171 *"raving cladists"*: Ibid., 240. See also p. 7.

171 *"numerical taxonomy"*: Ibid., 202.

172 *"shared evolutionary* novelties": Ibid., 251.

172 *a bat might look like a winged rodent*: R. J. Asher, N. Bennett, and T. Lehmann, "The New Framework for Understanding Placental Mammal Evolution," *Bioessays* 31, no. 8 (Aug. 2009): 853–64; H. Amrine-Madsen, K. P. Koepfli, R. K. Wayne, and M. S. Springer, "A New Phylogenetic Marker, Apolipoprotein B, Provides Compelling Evidence for Eutherian Relationships," *Molecular Phylogenetics and Evolution* 28, no. 2 (Aug. 2003): 225–40; Darren Naish, "The Refined, Fine-Tuned Placental Mammal Family Tree," *Scientific American*, July 14, 2015.

172 *more closely related to animals*: Patricia O. Wainright, Gregory Hinkle, Mitchell L. Sogin, and Shawn K. Stickel, "Monophyletic Origins of the Metazoa: An Evolutionary Link with Fungi," *Science*, Apr. 16, 1993, 340–42.

172 *"the ritual killing of the fish"*: Yoon, *Naming Nature*, 252.

173 *"show you exactly why you were wrong"*: Ibid., 254.

173 *"all the animals with red spots on them"* . . . *"or all the mammals that are loud"*: Ibid., 8.

176 *"Probably not"*: Author interview, David Smith, Feb. 28, 2017.

176 *"That's broadly accepted"*: Author interview, Melanie Stiassny, March 9, 2017.

176 *"It's counterintuitive!"*: Author interview, Dec. 12, 2017.

176 *the incredible medical case of J.B.R.*: Richard Greenwood, Ashok Bhalla, Alan Gordon, and Jeremy Roberts, "Behaviour Disturbances During Recovery from Herpes Simplex Encephalitis," *Journal of Neurology, Neurosurgery, and Psychiatry* 46 (1983): 809–17.

177 *differentiating between cats and dogs*: Lisa Oakes, Infant Cognition Lab, University of California, Davis.

177 *"I found it particularly painful"*: Yoon, *Naming Nature*, 252, 259.

180 *When Carol Kaesuk Yoon gave up the fish*: Ibid., 286–99.

180 *"It's been a constant battle"*: Author interview, Dec. 12, 2017.

181 *When Anna gave up the fish*: Author interview, March 20, 2017.

181 *When ethologist Jonathan Balcombe gave up the fish*: Author interview, March 19, 2019.

181 *differentiate between Bach and the blues*: Jonathan Balcombe, *What a Fish Knows: The Inner Lives of Our Underwater Cousins* (New York: *Scientific American*/Farrar, Straus and Giroux, 2016), 46.

181 *"kissing"* . . . *"linguistic castration"*: Frans de Waal, "What I Learned from Tickling Apes," *New York Times*, Apr. 8, 2016.

Epilogue

186 *"There is another world, but it is in this one"*: W. B. Yeats as cited in Sherman Alexie, *The Absolutely True Diary of a Part-Time Indian* (New York: Little, Brown and Company, 2007), epigraph.

191 *On Neptune, it rains diamonds*: Dominik Kraus, "On Neptune, It's Raining Diamonds," *American Scientist*, Sept. 2018, 285.

191 *the "interstitium"*: Rachael Rettner, "Meet Your Interstitium, a Newfound 'Organ,'" *Live Science*, March 27, 2018, https://www.livescience.com/62128-interstitium-organ.html.

194 *beat a black man bloody*: Ian Shapira, "The Parking Garage Beating Lasted 10 Seconds. DeAndre Harris Still Lives with the Damage," *Washington Post*, Sep. 16, 2019.

194 *"just as a matter of science"*: Jason Kessler, "Jason Kessler on His 'Unite the Right' Rally Move to DC," *Morning Edition*, NPR, Aug. 10, 2018.

About the Author

Lulu Miller is a Peabody Award–winning science reporter who has been working in public radio for over fifteen years. She is the co-founder of NPR's *Invisibilia*, a show about the invisible forces that shape human behavior. She is also a frequent contributor to *Radiolab*. Her writing has been published in *The New Yorker*, *VQR*, *Orion*, *Electric Literature*, *Catapult*, and beyond. Her favorite spot on earth is Humpback Rocks.